Highly recommended! Power in experienced by women in leader through and demonstrates how the thrive through the unseen advantag
Packed with practical advice, we are shown how to avoid the 'curse of comparison', focusing instead on our superpowers and learning to build trust through wisdom and humility.
    Dame Alison Peacock, chief executive, Chartered College of Teaching

A book to be revisited time and time again when you're in need of inspiration and a personal backer in your corner. Regardless of whether you're just setting out or you're well on your way with your leadership journey, this book has real gems of insight as well as super-practical support.
    Sharon Davies, CEO, Young Enterprise

Indispensable for all aspiring female leaders, this addresses an unfulfilled need in an informative and readable style.
    Sir Peter Williams, former chairman and CEO, Oxford Instruments; first male patron of WISE

I wish I'd had this when I first started leading teams. This is a great guide for any new or early career female manager, written by someone who has proved in practice to be an exceptional leader. It sets out everything you need to consider as you grow and develop into a leadership role. It's a guide that you will come back to again and again for guidance when things don't go quite according to plan or as you face new and different challenges.
    Sharon Hague, managing director, School Assessment and Qualification, Pearson

Jenny Jarvis has written a book that every female leader should read. It is full of practical advice on the situations you'll face – read it and be bold!
    Jennifer Coupland, CEO, Institute for Apprenticeships and Technical Education

This is an innovative new book on leadership that effectively blends MBA-level content with real on-the-job executive experience. This very readable book aimed at female leaders provides thought-provoking content for any new or experienced leader who wants to improve their leadership effectiveness.

JC Townsend, president, Adecco Group UK and Ireland

For women, this should become the default leadership bible. It acts as the mentor so many smart, ambitious women yearn for but find it hard to find. It combines a strategic overview of leadership styles with a very pragmatic set of tools to bring them into action – effectively! It delves simply into the complexity of gender differences and why women need to understand the context they operate in and the reactions their default styles may elicit. Men interested in building balanced teams and 'gender bilingual' leadership styles will find this enlightening.

Avivah Wittenberg-Cox, CEO, 20-first

Full of sensible advice and confidence-boosting measures for women (that will work for men as well). It reminds us that if we do nothing we shouldn't expect to achieve change. Throughout my career – the last 45 years or so – there have been initiatives to increase the number of women in leadership positions, so by now this book should not be necessary. But sadly, it is. So read this book and be part of making change happen, for your career and for the benefit of society.

Baroness Brown of Cambridge, crossbench member of the House of Lords

Lead with Confidence

Essential skills and strategies to **succeed** and **shine** as a female leader

Jenny Jarvis

I am grateful for all the fantastic people I have met during my professional career who have enhanced my understanding and enabled me to develop as a leader. I am also fortunate to know many strong women who bring happiness to my life.

With thanks to my parents, who have always encouraged me and been my biggest cheerleaders, and to Richard, who has been motivating, supportive and a great sounding board to test ideas.

I also greatly appreciated the beautiful Keats Community Library in Hampstead, London, which provided me with a quiet and peaceful space to write.

This book is for the many amazing women out there who are embarking on their own leadership journey.

Lead with Confidence
ISBN 978-1-915483-58-4 (paperback)
ISBN 978-1-915483-59-1 (ebook)

Published in 2025 by Right Book Press
Printed in the UK

© Jenny Jarvis 2025

The right of Jenny Jarvis to be identified as the author of this work has been asserted in accordance with the Copyright, Designs and Patents Act 1988. A CIP record of this book is available from the British Library.

All rights reserved. No part of this book may be reproduced, stored in a retrieval system, or transmitted in any form or by any means, electronic, mechanical, photocopying, recording or otherwise, without the prior written permission of the copyright holder.

Contents

Foreword	ix
Introduction	1
Why a book like this is needed	2
What you'll find in this book	4
Being a female leader	6
Becoming heroes	6
1 Establishing yourself as a leader	7
What kind of leader do you want to be?	7
Your physicality	19
Day one mentality	23
Meeting your team and setting expectations	25
Building your confidence as a leader	37
Finding the right coach, mentor or champion	39
Chapter reflections	45
2 Leadership in practice	47
Establishing the operating framework for an effective team	47
Leading your first major initiative	56
Leading a working group on a sensitive topic	63
Dealing with your first board or departmental meeting	65
Dealing with key external stakeholders	68
Effective communication	72
Making decisions	76
Chapter reflections	85
3 Dealing with some of the early leadership challenges	87
Being undervalued or underestimated	87
How you value yourself	92
What to do if you doubt yourself – the imposter syndrome	95
How to answer if someone asks you inappropriate questions	98
Dealing with unexpected behaviours – politics with a small p	100
Chapter reflections	102

4 Leadership tactics — 103
- Tackling confrontation inside and outside your organisation — 103
- Building networks — 109
- The art of conversation — 112
- Handling dissenters, dementors and disrupters — 115
- Leading with influence — 117
- Prioritisation and delegation — 121
- Chapter reflections — 123

5 Managing others — 125
- Managing your manager — 125
- Managing other women — 128
- Managing men — 131
- Managing a strong team — 133
- Managing underperformance in your team — 136
- Managing the process of removing an employee — 140
- Managing and dealing with effective meetings — 143
- Chapter reflections — 146

6 Essential leadership skills — 147
- Negotiation framework — 148
- Trusting your gut — 151
- Maintaining your wellbeing — 153
- Leading change — 157
- Problem solving and creativity — 160
- My preferred go-to creative problem-solving techniques — 162
- Understanding cultural intelligence — 164
- Tools for team reflection and assessment — 167
- Helpful tool for team development days — 169
- Chapter reflections — 171

7 Your role in the context of organisational leadership — 173
- Organisational development stages and what they mean — 174
- Being part of an SLT — 177
- The organisation's operating manual — 178
- Considering challenges at different levels of the organisation — 183
- Organisational values and culture — 184
- Chapter reflections — 186

8 How your manager can help you — 187

Final reflections — 195
- A few words on female leadership challenges — 196

References — 199

Toolkits and frameworks list:

✵1: Leadership style summary framework	10
✵2: Leadership style assessment tool	13
✵3: Key questions to ask direct reports when you first meet them	27
✵4: Establishing how you will work well with your staff members	34
✵5: Being clear about how you like to engage with staff	34
✵6: Setting out what kind of leader you are	36
✵7: Introducing yourself to a champion	43
✵8: Managing a team on a contentious matter	51
✵9: Tools to enable diversity of thought in a team	53
✵10: Exploratory questions for a new initiative	57
✵11: The RACI model	59
✵12: Producing written findings following project assessments	63
✵13: Finding out about your organisation's approach to governance	65
✵14: Effective strategic partnership working	71
✵15: The five Vroom and Yetton decision-making styles	78
✵16: The diagnosis decision rules	79
✵17: Group decision making in online meetings	82
✵18: Creating the conditions for input to in-person meetings	83
✵19: Responding if your input has been overlooked in a meeting	90
✵20: Dealing with imposter syndrome	95
✵21: Responding to inappropriate questions	98
✵22: Working within a toxic workplace culture	101
✵23: A framework for approaching confrontation with a colleague	104
✵24: Handling confrontation with external stakeholders	107
✵25: Making the most of a conversation	114
✵26: Working with dissenters, dementors or disrupters	116
✵27: The 4 Ds prioritisation tool	121
✵28: Managing your manager considerations	126
✵29: Handling the process of firing someone	141
✵30: Steering a new conversational direction	145
✵31: The negotiation toolkit	149
✵32: The stress bucket	154
✵33: Team adaptability and resilience framework	157
✵34: Problem-solving steps	160
✵35: Team vulnerability to aid problem solving	161
✵36: Team contribution assessment tool	167
✵37: Away day design framework	169
✵38: The organisational operating manual – the company car	182
✵39: Levels of organisational analysis – the SOGI model	183
✵40: Engaging your manager in supporting you	188

Foreword

Good leadership inside organisations is, in my 35+ years' experience, sadly not the norm, which is why I left large corporates in order to help them change by being an outsider. And I only could have done this by building confidence.

Having had very few informal mentors and even fewer role models early in my career made this challenging as there weren't as many women in senior roles in the late 1980s as there are now.

As a mentor and advisor to professional women – whether young female founders or senior women in board roles in companies of all sizes – who are advancing inside and outside formal organisations, this work is personal for me and very important, not least because our daughter is early in her professional career where the leaders above her could be giving her even more confidence.

So it seems to me that to lead others well, you need to understand that its practice relies on relationships, inspiring others, developing others, earning their trust and bringing a strategy to life.

Women in – or aspiring to be in – leadership roles have faced numerous challenges, including corporate cultures heavily biased in favour of male behaviours, not having enough allies, mentors or role models, not being represented enough in STEM sectors and not seeing themselves portrayed as leaders in the online and offline media we consume.

Building the confidence of professional women so they can put themselves in positions to take on more responsibility relies on having these resources plus a practical guide like this book, which I wish I had had in the earlier phases of my career.

Having first met Jenny some years ago while I was running executive education courses to build the capabilities of leaders in the world of further education, I realised we share the goal of wanting to help women become more effective and visible leaders.

Given we need more female leaders who give their employers so many advantages – more empathetic and human cultures, more diverse points of view for better decision making, more profitability, more representation inside the business that mirrors their markets served amongst many others – there's no better time than the present to grow a larger and wider pool of female talent.

While there are many books on leadership for women filled with a range of academic theories, I'm not aware of any that provide a thorough compendium of practical tools to build confidence or scenarios you'll likely encounter as you grow into bigger roles with more responsibility.

Jenny has created a unique and valuable handbook that's an accessible ready-reference handbook of effective tools and frameworks that build your excitement and confidence so you can put yourself in the way of opportunity far more often.

Across your journey as the reader, you'll encounter ideas that help you reflect on the leader you wish to be, the scenarios you'll doubtless encounter along the way, some of the challenges that will emerge and tactics you can deploy to help you navigate them successfully.

Because of Jenny's own lived experience as a leader, her work to campaign for more female leaders and her extensive research conducted with professional women, she's the right person to create this book with her encouraging voice infused across these pages.

Her desire to help even more women to be effective leaders is genuine, with a book that hopefully emboldens you, lifts you and helps you create change while amplifying the voices of all women in their pursuit of leadership roles.

It's my hope that *Lead with Confidence* provides you with reassurance, excitement and a mindset for self-belief as you continue building your leadership skills and set your sights on more responsibility and visibility.

Yours is a very exciting journey because leadership opportunities are all around you waiting to be seized. Choosing which to pursue will be driven by the people who will route resources to you, the people who will teach you what 'good' leadership is and the people who believe in you.

So I hope you enjoy the following pages as much as I have and that you look forward to seizing the chances to further build your leadership capabilities.

Allyson Stewart-Allen
CEO, International Marketing Partners

Introduction

If you are reading this book, you are on a leadership journey.

You may not feel ready, or even like a leader, but you must have reached a point in your career where others can see in you those essential qualities that will help you to thrive in a leadership role.

You might have just been appointed to a new leadership position or have a strong sense that you are destined to be a leader in the future. By picking up this book, not only are you making a commitment to yourself that you want to invest in your development, but you are also signalling your readiness for the journey you are on.

It is likely you will be feeling a mixture of emotions. You may be excited, but possibly not sure about what to do next. You could be doubting yourself and wondering why you are being viewed as a leader or potential leader. Through this book, I am here to be your coach, companion and cheerleader on your journey, whatever stage you are at.

I was 23 when I had my first national role, running European-funded programmes for an employment company. I remember feeling those exact mixed emotions. Just two years earlier, I had started my professional career as a temporary administrator. Through demonstrating capability and commitment, and because of two leaders who believed in me (thank you, Debbie and John), in a relatively short time I was appointed into a national role. I remember feeling confident, as this felt exactly right and where I should be; I knew my subject and had the backing of my managers. At the same time, I also felt an early sense of imposter syndrome – not helped by being asked several times by colleagues, 'How old are you, again?'

That swing between confidence and doubt has continued throughout every role but has become less of an issue. One reason is that my coping strategies have developed. The other is that I have built my leadership toolkit, which I am sharing with you here.

I would like to make several promises to you. By reading this book, you will learn about the most recognised leadership styles and be able to choose which one will work best for you. You will understand more about the subtle side of leadership and get help with how to respond to some of the challenges that leadership brings. You will be equipped with a variety of tools and frameworks to help you handle essential leadership tasks such as undertaking negotiation, tackling confrontation, leading change and handling those who disagree with your direction. I am also going to share with you insider tips for all the different types of 'management' you will encounter in your role, and I will help you by situating what it means to be a leader in the context of wider organisational leadership. I know that 23-year-old me would have benefited from this content, as I am sure you will too.

Why a book like this is needed

It is my contention that there is not enough shared belief or appreciation that females can be great leaders; however, my concern is that the specific contributions that women can make to organisations, society and world leadership are vital now more than ever.

We must address this, and this book is designed to do just that. It does so by myth busting, and by providing insights, tools and support to help more women have the confidence and belief that they can be successful in leadership roles.

I especially believe that a practical book is essential as a lot of leadership books can be quite theoretical, and while that may be appropriate for some leaders, for those taking their first leadership step, they need something more.

Over my 20 years in leadership roles, I've often been asked for advice on challenges such as how to handle confrontation, or what to do if you are undervalued by a colleague, or what type of leadership style might be appropriate. These questions were raised by women seeking answers to help them, but uncertain about their capability to lead, despite the fact that they were highly competent, inspirational and intelligent. They have all the raw materials; they just need assistance.

This is where my book comes in. After years of senior leadership roles where I have been fortunate to spend time developing colleagues and leading teams, I have managed to collate a multitude of useful tips and hints. These come not just from my own experience, but from the learning I have gained from other female leaders across multiple sectors. The conclusion I have come to over the years, and what drove me to write this book, is that I believe that what would help new female leaders most is to give them an advantage: access to the most helpful tools, language and frameworks required for success.

This book is grounded in years of research, practical experience and multiple business school courses, including an MBA at Warwick Business School, Finance for Non-Finance Executives at London Business School and the Preparing for CEO programme at Oxford's Saïd Business School. I'm also an advocate of peer learning, and my leadership thinking is therefore enhanced by insights gleaned from attending cross-sector leadership conversations with, for example, the Society of Leadership Fellows at Windsor, Ginger Leadership Communications and the Gordon

Book Conversations. This book distils what I have discovered from my experience, refined from my reading and learning, enhanced by peer input and brought together here for the first time. Many fantastic female leaders (and a few amazing male leaders, too!) have been willing to share their advice, which you will find dotted throughout this book. I have also referenced insightful authors where I feel this would be helpful. My first recommendation for women who want to be brave, be bold, choose courage over comfort and lead effectively is *Dare to Lead* by Brené Brown. You will find details of all references in the final pages.

What you'll find in this book

You can engage with this book in different ways, according to your needs. As an aspiring female leader or someone who knows they will be starting a leadership role, you could read from start to finish to help you prepare for those critical first few weeks and months. For a leader already in a new role, it offers a decisive pick-and-mix resource where you can turn to a relevant chapter whenever you need to. For the more established leader, it can act as a series of first principles that you can return to as a refresher whenever the demand arises.

The eight chapters will guide you through your journey, starting with how to prepare before you even begin your role, moving on to content that will help you develop your skills, competencies and understanding and your ability to respond effectively to a range of leadership challenges. The book ends with a framework to help your manager support you as a leader.

- → Chapter 1 focuses on how to establish yourself as a leader, helping you to think about what kind of leader you want to be. This is still relevant even if you are receiving a promotion at your current organisation.
- → Chapter 2 starts to explore what it means to act as

Introduction

a leader in practice and covers some of the naturally occurring activities or events you will need to deal with.
→ In Chapter 3, I talk about some of the behaviours and more delicate or complex experiences you may encounter. This includes some of the early emotive and potentially personal leadership challenges you may face.
→ Chapter 4 covers leadership tactics, looking at a range of practical areas where you will need to demonstrate leadership, such as tackling confrontation inside and outside your organisation and how to build networks.
→ Chapter 5 moves on to management in its many forms and considers managing upwards, sideways and down.
→ As a leader, you will need to have your own inbuilt set of mechanisms and tools for handling challenges. In Chapter 6, I talk through the essential leadership skills you will need to have in place to be effective.
→ Chapter 7 switches the focus to help you situate your role in the context of organisational leadership.
→ Chapter 8 reflects on the subjects covered in the previous seven, with the aim of assisting you to help your manager support you as a leader.
→ Throughout the chapters you will find useful tools, frameworks, reflection points and practical tips, alongside case studies and insights from other (predominantly female) leaders. Look out for the following symbols:

 Advice, guidance and case studies from other leaders.

 Self-reflection questions for you to consider.

 Tools, hints and tips.

Being a female leader

Before we get into the detail of this book, you may wonder why this isn't a general guide for *all* new leaders. There are some uniquely female challenges I am aiming to address through this book, so my intention has been to provide insights, suggestions and recommendations *as if I am advising or supporting female colleagues*. At the close of the book, I explore in more detail the uniquely female leadership challenges women face to help explain the rationale for this focus.

I also want to acknowledge that there are generalisations I make about male and female attributes in this book. The stance I take here draws from what I have experienced and has been shared with me by other female leaders, but, as with all generalisations, they can be inaccurate, especially in the complex gender identity landscape about which society is becoming more aware and educated.

Becoming heroes

I set out earlier my view that there is a lack of conviction that females can be great leaders. I firmly believe that only bold women can change that. I hope that through perseverance, peer support, women raising up other women, women demonstrating their capability and competence so that female leadership credentials are not in doubt (and indeed that female leadership qualities are recognised and revered), and through women enabling themselves through this type of learning, that women will be the heroes of their own leadership stories and of other women's leadership journeys too. Let's begin!

1 Establishing yourself as a leader

The idea of being prepared was something I learnt at an early age from after-school activities (Girl Guides and music exams) and from the role modelling of well-organised women in my family. It is no surprise then that I put a lot of preparation and thinking into new roles, such as doing research on the team, the company, the board and chair, or thinking through how I am going to approach the role. It is also unsurprising that this book begins with a focus on getting you ready for your role before you have even started it. In working through this chapter, you will consider what kind of leader you want to be, think about your leadership physicality, prepare your day one mentality, get ready to meet your team and reflect on how you will build your confidence as a leader.

What kind of leader do you want to be?

You will frequently be asked which style you apply to your leadership. This is a common interview question, so it is good to understand the variety of styles and your preferred approach to give the best answer in that instance. However, it is even more important to be clear on this for yourself – in part because it helps to present a consistent version of you to others, so that they know what to expect in terms of how you will behave and operate. It is also a reality that you will face challenging situations in work and will need to respond in the best way you can, which may mean adopting the most appropriate leadership style suited to that situation.

A leadership style is about demonstrating your approach and the likely associated behaviour when you are leading and managing others. It is not just a reflection of how you will go about directing and engaging with staff; it also indicates how you will interface with the company and wider stakeholders, how much autonomy you will hand to others and how close you will be to the detail of the organisation's activities.

Identifying what your leadership style is, and then demonstrating that style through how you operate, enables others to work effectively with you and vice versa. How others respond to you may also be a useful guide to whether you are operating or behaving in line with how you want to be perceived. For example, if you wish to be known as a 'democratic' leader (see definitions below), but employees provide feedback that they are working in a team where their ideas are not heard and where they do not get a chance to provide input or expertise, then you might need to examine what is going wrong and see where you could make adjustments.

There are many ways of describing the different types of leadership styles, with numerous specialists summarising their own interpretations of the different approaches. Categorisations I have found useful include the framing from Braden Becker, a senior SEO strategist for HubSpot, who references (among other styles) 'strategic leadership', where leaders position themselves as balanced between a company's primary operations and its growth opportunities; 'transformational leaders' who gain the trust and confidence of their teams and aim to inspire and motivate staff in order to achieve change; 'transactional leaders' who tell their staff exactly what they want them to do and then motivate them by using rewards or benefits; and 'situational leaders' who change their management style to meet the needs of the situation or team.

I also like the framing by recruitment website Indeed, which lists eight styles, including autocratic, bureaucratic, coaching, democratic, laissez-faire, pacesetter, servant and visionary leadership. The one style I wish to expand on from this list is 'servant leadership', as this is a popular term being used to signify leaders who demonstrate a people-first mindset, believing that when team members feel personally and professionally fulfilled, they are more effective and more likely to regularly produce great work.

In considering the descriptors to share with you, I felt that the categories outlined by Daniel Goleman in *Harvard Business Review* (2000) were particularly useful, as they reflect the best examples of less commonly used terminology and capture some of the subtle nuances I have seen reflected in the range of leaders I have met. The six styles are described as:

1. **Commanding.** The leader demands immediate compliance and the respondent should do what the leader tells them. This style is best adopted in a crisis scenario or to address an issue with problem employees. Overall, this can have a negative impact on culture.
2. **Visionary.** This style mobilises people towards a vision. It encourages staff to come with the leader on a journey and is appropriate when there are changes being made or a new direction is needed. It can have a positive impact on culture.
3. **Affiliative.** This style creates harmony and builds emotional bonds. It's when the leader puts people first and is useful when there's a need to heal rifts in a team or motivate people during difficult circumstances.
4. **Democratic.** This style achieves consensus through the participation of others in decisions or activities. It gets buy-in and input from others and seeks out their opinions. This approach is useful when a leader needs to

build agreement and can have a positive cultural impact.
5. **Pacesetting.** When a leader sets high standards for performance. This often involves role modelling or 'follow me' demonstration. This works when you need to get good or quick results from a strong team. It can have negative implications for culture if staff struggle to be led this way or meet the standards that have been set out.
6. **Coaching.** When a sympathetic environment is in place, where staff are developed and encouraged to try new approaches or supported to deliver what needs to be achieved. This approach helps improve employee performance over the long term and has a positive impact on culture.

As you can see, there are many ways of framing the numerous types of leadership styles, which can cause confusion. There are also slight variations in what the terms mean between the different authors and academics. To help with this, the first tool I am going to share with you groups these styles into four categories. I have drawn this together through detailed mapping and reflection on the wealth of styles and framing I have come across, considering what each style really delivers and how it correlates with other similar styles.

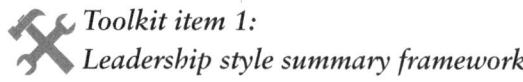
Toolkit item 1:
Leadership style summary framework

Directional leaders. For this type of leader, you might also apply the headings of autocratic, commanding, pacesetting, transactional or bureaucratic. For me, it is those who roll up their sleeves, set out the processes they want to be followed, direct from the front, probably do less to empower others with flexibilities or freedoms, and give less autonomy to their staff, taking a more directive approach in framing what needs to be delivered. As a generalisation, these leaders can sometimes forget the human element of their responsibilities but can be highly effective in achieving results and team efficiency.

Supportive leaders. The coaching, democratic and servant leaders. These leaders operate with a focus on people first and recognise the longer-term benefit of gaining the trust and respect of staff to achieve goals. They are often empathetic leaders who can help others achieve their potential. Sometimes, if they always look to ensure consensus or buy-in before taking decisions, this could undermine their leadership credibility.

Transformational leaders. Strategic and visionary leaders: those who lead from the front, boldly setting out what they are looking to achieve, encouraging others to embrace their vision, clearly articulating both the change and what that change will bring to all stakeholders. They may not appreciate the change fatigue or caution some display in response to this style.

Ambassadorial leaders. A category that laissez-faire leaders fit into. Those who essentially stand further back from the action (organisational design, delivery and operating model), who perhaps enjoy the more external-facing elements of their work (figureheads or brand representatives), and who give a lot of autonomy to their staff but may not necessarily provide the fully supportive environment needed to ensure that staff are able to succeed. This style can work well for a CEO if the organisation has an empowered deputy, DCEO or COO who can take more of a direct role in leading the business.

Although you may settle on one or more ways of leading that best fit with both your character and the situational context in which you operate, it is highly likely that you will experience circumstances which demand that a particular style be incorporated into your approach to address the situation you face. This may or may not be the style you ordinarily apply and might only be for a fixed period. For example, a crisis (such as the Covid-19 pandemic) may precipitate a need to use a 'commanding' leadership style to ensure that a level of direction setting and control is in place, that compliance is enforced and that staff respond to directives from leaders in a timely manner.

It might be that some styles are less well received when adopted by women than by men and that perceptions about how women behave and how that aligns with leadership might be a challenge to be aware of. For example, when I think about traits often associated with female leadership, I imagine they are less likely to be linked with the Directional and Transformational leadership styles I describe below and could more closely be associated with Supportive or Ambassadorial leaders instead.

In addition, how women or men actually behave can also have an impact on their perceived effectiveness. Research based on a series of studies conducted by Dr Joyce Bono (Bono et al 2017) investigating associations among 'gender, interpersonal behaviours, and derailment' examined negative derailing behaviours, such as talking over someone or forging ahead without getting others on board with your plans. In the study, managers were assessed by their leaders. It was concluded that those who demonstrated ineffective interpersonal behaviours were more likely to derail their colleagues. That is not too surprising; however, what was interesting is that the correlation between these negative behaviours and their ability to derail colleagues was significantly stronger for women. Essentially, behaving badly at work has more serious consequences for women. I most closely associate the possibility for these behaviours to be displayed with being

Establishing yourself as a leader

a Directive leader, where you set direction in a decisive way which could involve derailing behaviours. However, there are ways to be decisive without acting badly or treating colleagues with disrespect.

The thoughts shared here shouldn't change what style you generally adopt or apply as required in specific scenarios, but perceptions about female behaviour and how you act when adopting certain leadership styles are useful to be aware of when considering how you lead.

The following tool will help you assess where you are now and consider how to move to the style you need to adopt.

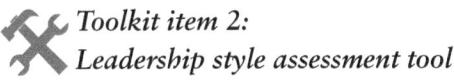

Toolkit item 2:
Leadership style assessment tool

Reflect on the following to consider where you currently are and where you want to be.

Directional leader
How to know you adopt this style:
You like setting direction and leading from the front. You prefer to set the pace and standards of the work. You get directly involved in designing and shaping the work that will be delivered. You provide less space for others to choose how they will undertake the activity. You are results focused and like achieving success and having personal responsibility for overseeing the organisational delivery.

How to become more like this style:
If this is not naturally how you operate, but a situation means you need to adopt a more directive approach, I would suggest:

→ Don't be afraid to take control of the situation, particularly if there is a crisis being addressed. People will

expect that a leader will do this given the context, even if that is not their natural style.
→ Be prepared to issue instructions in a clear and concise way.
→ Reflect on your leadership physicality (see page 19) and what you may need to change to embody this leadership style.
→ Articulate the standards you wish to see adhered to.
→ Create a structure for operating, including using the RACI model to be clear on accountability (see page 59).

Supportive leader
How to know you adopt this style:
You like working with others and prioritise gaining trust and understanding the capabilities and skillsets of your team to best work with them to achieve organisational goals. You enjoy coaching and mentoring others and are excited to help colleagues fulfil their potential. You support group working and aim to achieve consensus on decision making where you can. You recognise that a team is made stronger by the relative strengths within it, and you enjoy working with colleagues who have skillsets and knowledge you do not possess, making you stronger as an overall group.

How to become more like this style:
To become a more supportive leader if this is not natural to you:

→ Take time to understand your team. Ask how you might help them to develop their strengths further and address their weaknesses.
→ Find out about their ambitions and goals, and see whether they have any hidden talents or skills that

they may be able to bring to enhance the work of the team.
→ Consider how specific pieces of work might provide opportunities for your team to deploy or develop their expertise.
→ Get professional help to assist you in developing your coaching style.
→ Explore the decision-making styles (see page 78) and consider whether you reflect sufficiently on decision acceptance in your approach.

Transformational leader

How to know you adopt this style:
You are someone who thinks strategically and likes to articulate your vision and share that with others. You can imagine what your change will achieve. You like to engage others in the vision that you are setting out. You likely have high energy and are perceived to be an extrovert (even if you are not).

How to become more like this style:
If you need to act as a transformational leader, you might like to:

→ Spend time developing a vision statement and test it with trusted colleagues.
→ Ensure that your vision will engage others: make sure it is not too complex but that it explains the benefits of the transformation and tells a story that others will understand.
→ Create change agents: those who will enthuse and excite others (see 'Leading change' on pages 157–9).
→ Make sure you communicate expectations clearly.
→ Provide a sense of purpose to your team. Consider what engages and inspires them to work hard and

achieve great results, and draw on those elements in how you shape the work that is required.

Ambassadorial leader

How to know you adopt this style:
You will likely operate slightly at arm's length from the detail and prefer considering the bigger picture. You like representing your team and your work externally and enjoy championing the brand or organisation. You will empower your team and trust them to deliver what is needed and would rather not be too prescriptive on the detail of how that work needs to happen.

How to become more like this style:
If you need to act like more of an ambassadorial leader, you could:

→ Understand from marketing colleagues what the key external messages are and how you should be framing them.
→ Ask how you can play a role in promoting the company – online, at events, at conferences.
→ Use company brand language in internal and external meetings.
→ Learn how to network effectively (see page 109).
→ Let your team know you trust them to deliver and that they have accountability for leading the work. On this point, I would suggest that you also tell them this doesn't mean that they hold off on escalating any issues to you should the need arise.

Having spent nearly 20 years leading and directing, I have thought a lot about my personal style and how I want to lead others. I aspire to demonstrate a combination of being a supportive (servant) leader alongside being a transformational leader. I care about what staff think, can recognise that their expertise will add value to my work and feel it is important to act as both a facilitator and enabler of success in others. I combine this care with boldness about how and when to take leadership decisions, aiming to deliver clarity to colleagues and empower others to take an active part in the fulfilment of any vision.

However, we all have off days, and I am certain I don't always live up to that style. As much as I might like to think that I come across in a certain way, there may be a gap between the style I think I'm adopting and the style I'm seen to demonstrate by others. This highlights the importance of having heightened levels of awareness about how we come across.

Further feedback from my professional peer group on this leadership taxonomy included an insightful perspective from a male colleague from the Society of Leadership Fellows. He shared that for him, there is something new and emerging about leadership which comes from difference and/or a lack of privilege. This is a group of people for whom opportunities to lead felt furthest away and who found it hard or impossible to find leaders who looked like them or had similar lived experience. This is a relevant and essential insight not only about how leadership rightly evolves but also reminds us of the importance of having diversity in role models to inspire future generations of leaders.

It is great that as a leadership community and society, we keep redefining and challenging the established leadership styles and that new ideas emerge, moving away and evolving from the early leadership theories such as the 'great man' theory (a view that some people are just born with characteristics that naturally make them skilled leaders) and trait theory (an approach to the study of human personality, focused on the measurement of 'traits', defined as patterns of behaviour, thought and emotion). For staff in professional communities, it is important to see a wider variety of styles adopted and practised, and adaptations made which ensure that leadership approaches are fit for purpose for the modern-day workforce.

This is an ongoing debate, and it is helpful to keep up to date with what the latest thinking is, if only to ensure you are using the right terminology to articulate how you lead. It is also important to think beyond styles when considering how to behave and respond as a leader. One way to do this is by reflecting on your core values. As Amanda shares:

My personal values are probably the chief influencer over my style, but [it is key that they are] reflecting both the circumstances and how successfully our activities are aligned with purpose.
Amanda Melton, CBE, Independent leadership coach

Having read through this section, and applied the leadership style assessment tool, what are your thoughts on what kind of leader you are or want to be?

It might be worth asking peers what kind of leader they think you are, to test whether this matches your preferred style.

Your physicality

What does a leader look and sound like? Well, this question is probably a bit daft as there is no one correct answer and, over time, the typical look and feel of a leader has changed so dramatically. Just think how different leaders look from the era of Henry Ford (1863–1947), a revolutionary in his time and probably both a transformational and directive leader, who was always smartly suited and booted, compared to leaders today such as Sarina Wiegman, the England women's football team manager from 2021, who leads from the side of the pitch in a tracksuit and operates a supportive, directive and also encouraging style.

We have leaders of all ages, genders, looks and abilities. That is a great thing. However, there are still physical aspects it is helpful to consider when establishing your leadership presence. I heard advice years ago that when leading others, it is important to 'lead yourself first', and that it's possible to make the best use of your body and think about how you control your physicality to give you confidence. This, in turn, means others will be likely to have confidence in you.

Stance

There is an abundance of literature and evidence from places such as the Mayo Clinic and Harvard Medical School on the importance of having a strong core, good posture and feeling physically grounded. Practices like yoga and Pilates teach the benefits of strengthening our bodies to be able to brace ourselves for challenges. In a movement class, we might be invited to imagine a piece of string pulling up from the top of our head to help us (if we are able) sit or stand up tall and elongate our posture. I have also received great advice over the years about the importance of not just being a grounded leader (listening to staff and trying to have a low ego) but to also try to be physically grounded. I have found this especially useful when I have had to give a speech or present an award and felt my legs or body shaking through nerves. Imagining strong roots growing deep into the earth gives me balance and anchors me effectively. Thinking about posture and grounding when presenting yourself to others gives an appearance of confidence and strength.

Breath

The power of the breath should not be underestimated. Breath can be used, among other things, to ease tension, calm anxiety, control our response and voice and help us to gain composure. I recommend you find some breathing techniques that work for you and think about how you can turn that practice into a regular habit that you can adopt when you need it most. You could also use mindfulness videos or apps such as Headspace or Calm. A good calming breathing technique I have found beneficial is the simple 4–4–4 count. Breathe in for the count of four, hold your breath for four seconds and breathe out evenly for four more seconds. Then rest and repeat. Just focusing on your breathing and being mindful will help to create a sense of calm.

Voice

For many of us, if we are prepared to admit it, there are some voices that might inspire greater confidence and credibility than others. I remember people joking about David Beckham's voice when he was younger but look at all he has achieved! So, what can help? Using your breath well, as far as you can, really helps you to have a steadier and more controlled voice, enabling you to speak calmly and exude an air of confidence.

In an exercise on a business school course I was on, a lecturer made a simple observation: if you rush to answer a phone and pick up the receiver straight away, the pitch of your voice is often quite high (imagine a rather breathy and high-pitched 'hello'). However, if instead you take a pause and a deep breath and let it out steadily, then answer the phone, you can end up an octave lower in your response pitch. This is relevant, as in general, studies show that a confident voice is lower and controlled. This seems to generate greater credibility. If you are not confident in your speaking voice, you could consider elocution or enunciation lessons, doing a Toastmasters course, or having some speech therapy to work on your intonation and projection. Many well-established leaders do this.

Body language

Although this may not always be easy, I would recommend that you aim to outwardly project confidence through your body language. I like seeing leaders whose body language is open. The opposite of this would include simple things such as crossing your arms or legs or using your body to create a barrier between you and those with whom you are engaging – for example, turning your back on people. It is also worth remembering that a lot of communication is unspoken. Non-verbal messages can include how you move your body, the tone of your voice, your facial expressions and a range of other signals too.

Think about whether you might be inadvertently revealing what you are thinking through your physicality: do you wring your hands in anxiety, tap your foot in impatience, fiddle with your hair or furrow your brows when confused? What are your telltale signs? If you aren't sure, ask someone who knows you well!

What you wear

There is no fixed rule on dressing for work as context counts a lot. With increasingly flexible models of working, many would admit that they wear more casual attire for their home-working wardrobe. Whatever you find is appropriate for the nature of your work and the culture of the organisation you work in should be fine. I wouldn't recommend trying to make a statement you might regret through clothes or make-up. I've found it's best not to put on any pretences: aim to give the truest representation of yourself, as long as it is appropriate for the circumstances. Some companies will have a dress code you might need to adhere to. Check if this is the case for you.

Greeting

When you meet someone, how do you greet them? This is rather a minefield and can vary from a hand up to signal hello, a handshake, a kiss on the cheek (this seems more outdated these days) or, in some cultures, a bow or a nod. Knowing the cultural context is key – what is the custom where you work? I would argue that the most common professional greeting in the Western world is the handshake. When greeting someone this way, avoid too much hesitation and look them in the eye, stick out your hand to greet them with open body language and a smile. This has worked well for me. Some people find it awkward to decide how to greet other people, so you will get extra credit for initiating. A good amount of firmness in your grip is also important.

This may all seem like a lot to consider. But it is worth it. Let's be honest, few of us would feel too enthusiastic about following a leader who curls themselves into a ball, looks at the ground when speaking and mumbles. Hold your head high, practise your composure and be warm and open, and you will do well.

Establishing yourself as a leader

Are there elements of your physicality you think are obvious areas you might like to work on? Where would you get the help and advice you need?

Day one mentality

Preparation for a new role as a leader has a lot to do with your mentality. Rather than fearing potential failure or worrying you might not be successful, start your first day, your first week and every month with a resolute belief that you can be, and are, a successful leader. Having a positive mindset from the outset will be important. Push away doubts about whether you should be a leader, quieten the noise in your head that could give you that anxiety and try to give yourself positive reinforcement.

Affirmations

One way I like to do this is by using affirmations, which are phrases that we choose to represent who we would like to become. At times in my career, I have found affirmations truly empowering. It's suggested that if you visualise your most successful self and life, write down what that looks like and repeat it to yourself (ideally out loud), you will start believing what you are hearing. A few years ago, I spent some time thinking about affirmations, and once I had my list, I trained myself to repeat them daily. I was able to use these affirmations as a source of confidence and to remind me of my strengths. My list included:

→ I am a superhero (because, let's face it, women are the heroes of their leadership stories!).
→ I am not weighed down by any previous baggage. (I said

this to myself every day because I wanted to wipe the slate clean of any issues from the past.)
→ I will remind myself of my why. (Simon Sinek is a great author who asks us to think about our 'why' – our reasons for doing what we do. It is a powerful driver.)
→ I will tackle confrontations. (I find this challenging, so I wanted to commit every day that I would tackle issues as they arose.)
→ I will remember that if nothing changes, nothing changes. (I know I have to take action in order to make a difference and to reveal new possibilities.)
→ Today is the only day we have. (We don't have yesterday and don't yet have tomorrow, so make the utmost of today.)
→ I deserve an extraordinary life. (This is about tackling that imposter in your head. You do deserve this!)

Making a difference from day one

I was speaking to a friend who was starting a role and we were reflecting on what it is that gets someone noticed (for the right reasons) when they begin a new job. My conclusion is that it's the person who has the mindset to go above and beyond expectations on both big and small tasks from day one. For example, if you were asked to produce a report rather than just delivering it on time, what about also providing additional information and guidance, situating your report in a wider context, or asking whether it might be useful to turn it into a presentation that could be shared more widely?

An ex-colleague once said to me, if you can get a halo above your head in the first month of starting a role, people will remember that, and as long as you don't make any massive errors, it will remain there. Essentially, the first impressions you make at work count – and last. I'd like to stress that there's a difference between this and someone who spends time trying to obviously flatter other leaders. That behaviour will be viewed as insincere and could cause frustration, but being excellent, going the extra mile and adding value should not.

Set the tone

It is also advisable to set the tone for how you will operate from day one. For example, make sure you do what you say you are going to do and manage expectations, especially if there is any reason you can't meet a deadline or complete a task. I would also advise you to take a genuine interest in the work you do, your colleagues, your company and your team. You could allow a childlike sense of curiosity to be a part of how you operate – especially when you are new in a role. You should have permission to ask lots of questions about why things are the way they are. There is a small window when you start a role for some of those questions, so make sure you take the chance, listen, take notes and explore further when you can.

Meeting your team and setting expectations

There is a difference between meeting your team when you don't know them or are new to a company and meeting your team when you know some of them, or you currently work at the same place. You will need to take a slightly different approach according to the circumstances.

Meeting your team when you don't know them

When you join a new organisation as a leader, in this age of social media, you are likely to find colleagues who have researched your background and what skills and experience you will bring. Even if individuals haven't done any research, it is likely they will still have expectations about what you will be like (perhaps, unfortunately, what you will look like, how old you are and what background you will come from), and you may or may not match those preconceptions. There may also be staff in the company who applied for your role and were unsuccessful. There is nothing you can do to change any of this, so don't worry; these issues can quickly be addressed by how you interact with your colleagues from the outset.

So, how do you get started? My advice is that if possible and appropriate, you might wish to make contact with key team members, or the whole team, before you begin. This may be a brief note to say that you are delighted to be taking on your new role, that your aim is to meet with everyone shortly after you start and you are looking forward to working with them. This can work well, but may not always be appropriate, so do check. It also may not be possible to 'meet with everyone' individually if you are joining a larger organisation, so be careful what you commit to.

If you have line management responsibilities, getting insight on your team in advance is helpful. Ask for HR profiles, performance and development records, team structures, organograms and other information. You can use these to understand more about the roles and colleagues you will be working with, and also get an understanding of how staff have been performing. Be careful not to pre-judge capabilities or competencies for those individuals, though: this HR information provides some context, but you will need to form your own views once you meet your team.

Finding out (if your line manager is able to share) if anyone applied for your role is helpful, too, so you can add further insight to any behaviours that staff may display towards you. However, I would not recommend mentioning to the individual that you know this. Leave it to them to say if they want to; otherwise, just be aware that some of their reactions to you may be influenced by this fact.

It is important to meet your team early in your role.

When you do, whether you are a line manager or joining a team as a peer, it is essential that you take time to actively listen to colleagues, ask them some key questions to explore how things are going and learn more about them, and share insights about yourself to start building trust through forming a connection.

> **Toolkit item 3: Key questions to ask direct reports when you first meet them**
>
> In our first meeting, I like to ask colleagues four questions:
>
> 1. Tell me about your role (and team, if relevant) and what the main areas of focus are (essentially, what do you deliver/what function do you perform?).
> 2. What do you see as being the core strengths of your work?
> 3. Are there areas of your work where you have identified that there are currently weaknesses or areas for improvement?
> 4. In what way could I help make the biggest difference to your work or role?

You will notice that these questions are not necessarily personal – although people may choose to frame their responses that way. They are about 'the work'.

Usually, an induction will be planned for you. Make sure you have sessions booked in with all the key individuals in your team and, ideally, a chance to talk to the whole team together relatively early on. It is important to remember that in some companies, there may be a 'them and us' culture ('them' being managers or leaders, and 'us' being the rest of the staff). Where you can, showing that all staff matter to you can help make sure that you do not continue to foster that culture in your team.

When I joined a company in my late thirties – in the days when many staff were office-based – I had an organisation chart in front of me and I went and found every single person (holidays permitting) on the chart in my first three days and asked them about their role. I shared with them that I was willing to listen and keen to hear new ideas and get input. It seemed to go down well. I did the same at my first board meeting, approaching every board member. Again, this was well received, because I had shown willingness, openness and interest.

In your first few weeks, it is also helpful to introduce yourself to everyone you come across that you don't know. Being seen early on as approachable and willing to engage has always stood me in good stead. Not being selective about who you speak to is also important, as all staff should be valued.

It is well established that showing vulnerability and displaying openness and honesty will help build solid foundations of trust. However, you may wonder how much to share. I had a colleague who wisely said, 'Only share as much as you feel comfortable sharing.' Simple, but effective. I would add to that: be aware that what you reveal about yourself will be remembered and can't be unsaid. However, I wouldn't want to make anyone overly concerned, as bringing some of your personal life into work helps humanise you as a leader. In Chapter 3 (page 98), I talk more about how to handle inappropriate or overly personal questions.

Keeping track of staff priorities

From the outset, it is useful to keep track of what is happening with your team and items you want to discuss with them. My tip is to keep a log of a few key points, such as:

→ development areas being worked on (to be supportive of their progress)
→ challenges they are facing and working through (to hear

updates and see if I can assist in any way)
- → significant decisions they have made (to be able to ask them how that decision is working out)
- → key updates I want to share with them (information I think would be useful for them to know or ideas about how I might assist them with their work)
- → questions I want to ask (to resolve queries I have or to test items with them)
- → ideas for their development (to enhance their skills, knowledge or capabilities)
- → any tasks I want to assign to them (to share the detail and level of importance).

Keeping a running list of these items per staff member means I can discuss any of these matters with them when we next speak and won't lose track of important items I want to cover.

Meeting your team where you currently work

There are elements of the advice for joining a new organisation that I would also apply when you have been promoted in your current company, especially remembering that you may have colleagues who also went for your role, and you will want to be sensitive to that situation. The main difference is that you need to be clear to others through what you say and how you behave, that you are forming a new and different relationship with them.

You should take the lead in establishing this new relationship with colleagues, and I would suggest that a helpful first step is to acknowledge that there has been a change. You might do this at your first engagement with your staff (either on a one-to-one or team basis), by taking the time to express how pleased you are to have been awarded this leadership responsibility. You should add that you recognise things will be different, and although you are still colleagues, you have been asked to take on this role and are ready to shoulder the responsibilities that come with your new position, and that you will be keen to represent the team in the best possible light within the company.

Given the possibility that some or many members of your team will know you, but in a different capacity, you may need to reassure them that you are right for this role and/or that you will be an effective leader of the team. Doing this could take more than verbal assurances: people may need to be convinced over time by your actions, not just by your words.

In the first individual meetings with your team, you may wish to refer to the 'Key questions to ask direct reports' list on page 27, framing these by asking colleagues not to assume you know the answers and to try and respond as if you were new to the organisation. Hearing how staff describe their roles, their strengths, areas for improvement and how you could help will be insightful and useful as you start working together in this new way.

I spoke to a leader about a time when she experienced a step up at a company where she was already working, and she kindly provided this detail.

What was the situation?
There were two director jobs available and clear signals were provided that internal appointments would be preferred. There were five peers who applied for the roles, with four being taken through to the second interview stage. I'd say that I wasn't the favourite to get the role and that there was a certain element of surprise from people when I was successful.

What was the challenge you were facing?
I think it was establishing myself in a more senior level role, while at the same time dealing with the understandable disappointment from people who were previously my peers and with whom I'd got on well. While three of the four were gracious enough to congratulate me and one person was never anything other than extremely supportive, I felt very visible during the immediate period after I was promoted and aware that I was being discussed. The outgoing director made this more difficult in some ways by keeping me up to date with how people were feeling.

What approach did you take?
Essentially, I took the view that the only thing I could do was to get on and do the job to the best of my ability. I didn't apologise to anyone for getting the role that they had wanted, and I didn't attempt to discuss their feelings about it with them.

As this was my first senior leadership team (SLT) level position I had a lot to learn. It was very helpful that I was promoted with someone else who a) had more experience than me and b) was generous in sharing their expertise and in recognising and praising the skills and knowledge I had that they didn't. I also had an extremely supportive manager who gave me the help I needed and the time that I required to grow into the role.

I identified the areas where I felt more comfortable, which was about learning information about new programmes and establishing relationships with people and contractors I hadn't worked with directly before. I also learnt about where I needed to step up and do things differently, which was about thinking more strategically, taking more decisions, being visible in SLT meetings and not being worried about having a view that was different to that of other people.

It helped me to try and stay positive during the first weeks and to remember that the world moves on and that the people who were feeling resentful would either get over it or take the decision to leave. It was helpful that two of the people did decide to move on after a few months. It also helped that the role was busy from day one and a lot of that was about recruitment, which was positive as it involved bringing new people into the organisation who only knew me as 'the director'.

I'm not sure whether this is good advice or not, but I created a time limit to make a decision about the role. This helped me to remember that life is about more than work and that if the new job didn't work out then there would be other things I could do.

What did you learn?
The main things I took away from the experience included:
→ Your peer group changes when you're promoted. You can't have the same relationships when you're managing people as you did when you were their peer and trying to do this will usually result in difficulties. However, you gain a new peer group.
→ Most people don't cling on to feelings of resentment forever. Even the most bitter people usually get over the disappointment because it's in their own interest to do so.
→ Most people in the organisation, other than those people who had applied for the roles, probably didn't have a strong view about me getting promoted and so the visibility I felt at the start was in my head.
→ Identifying quick wins is important. These can be small things like being supportive to a new person

who you've taken on line management for or taking a decision that wasn't earth shattering but that helped someone move forward.
→ Take the time to listen to the people around you. There is a window where no one expects you to know everything and utilising this effectively can help ensure you are properly informed and is also great for building relationships.
→ This window exists even in organisations that have very high expectations for new staff and/or people in new roles. It can be helpful to remember that you're not expected to know everything from the start and that asking the right questions goes a long way to building credibility.
→ Identifying people to learn from and to bounce ideas off is important. For me this was my line manager as well as the person who was promoted at the same time as me, but it could be someone external to the organisation, including a more formal relationship such as a coach or mentor.
→ Ultimately, the importance of making the most of the opportunity. Being promoted within the same organisation brings different challenges to gaining promotion somewhere new. It's important to be brave, to accept that you're probably going to be out of your comfort zone and to focus on the positives.

A senior operations director

Setting expectations

Staff who work for you will look to you to understand how you will work together, how you like to engage with colleagues more widely, and what kind of leader you are. I have set out three suggested approaches to setting expectations.

> **⚒ Toolkit item 4: Establishing how you will work well with your staff members**
>
> *Setting: first one-to-one meeting with each individual staff member*
> A technique that works well is to explore three simple questions in your early engagement. These questions help establish boundaries and provide useful starting points for discussion:
>
> 1. How do you like to work?
> 2. How do I like to work?
> 3. How would we best work together?
>
> Your discussion prompts might include reflecting on communication preferences, the best ways to stay in touch, what kind of issues you will respectively share and/or want to hear about, information about working patterns and preferences, and any personal adjustments you want to make one another aware of. This is a chance to share some thoughts and insights to really get to understand each other better.

> **⚒ Toolkit item 5: Being clear about how you like to engage with staff**
>
> *Setting: your first team meeting*
> These fit with the questions above about how you like to work, but are relevant to how you will engage with staff more widely. Spend a little time thinking about your answers to the following questions to give you some ideas for information you can share about how you will operate:
>
> → What is the best way for your team to get in touch with you?

- → What communication tools would you like to use for the team?
- → If you have an office, will you be in it and how often? If not, when are the best times to contact you (if there is a need to establish this)?
- → Will you have a set working pattern and times you are available or periods when you would rather not be disturbed?
- → If staff are unsure whether an issue requires escalation to you, what should they do?
- → If your staff member tells you that a piece of work or their workload is unmanageable, how will you receive that news and what tone do you want to set with your team so that they feel comfortable to admit mistakes?
- → How will you share information?
- → If there is an urgent matter to be addressed, how do you want to hear about it and what response can staff expect from you?
- → Do you want colleagues to let you know if a request for your time is for decision making, sharing ideas or for information dissemination?

To give you some thoughts on answers to the above, I like to say that my (virtual) door is always open, I don't like surprises and would rather hear of issues as they arise, that I can be reached via direct messaging for issues that need escalation, otherwise I like to have one-to-ones to review performance and development on a fortnightly basis. I am happy to be a point of support and/or someone to bounce ideas off and am happy to be a decision maker where appropriate. I care about work–life balance and the wellbeing of my team and hope that staff will let me know if they feel they are overworked or struggling to handle their workload.

> **Toolkit item 6: Setting out what kind of leader you are**

Setting: circa one month in at a team meeting where you start to share more about your leadership approach and the direction for the team

Sharing this with staff is part of what helps to set expectations. Rather than describing a leadership style (pages 7–18), you might want to share what type of leader you are through some examples that provide insights into your leadership approach. I recommend doing this because not everyone buys into or cares about leadership styles as a concept, so just saying you are a 'servant leader' might not get you very far!

Some framing you could consider includes:

→ How others might experience your leadership style. For example, I like to lead in a way that means I hear from everyone when a decision impacts the whole team.
→ Your personal and motivational link to the organisational mission/vision and how you feel the team will contribute.
→ How you see the team working effectively and your role in that team, including sharing which areas you might contribute to more directly, and on what matters you are best placed to facilitate so you enable others to provide expertise.
→ Your decision-making style and how you reassure others that you are prepared to take necessary decisions (see page 76 for more on this).
→ How you came to the role you are in now, as sharing your leadership journey helps frame your approach.
→ Early thoughts on the direction that you wish to take the team in and your vision for how the team will achieve their goals under your leadership.

Building your confidence as a leader

Although I considered earlier the physical ways in which you can present yourself with confidence, in this section I want focus instead on a greater source of confidence: the strength that comes from within. Having inner courage and the mental strength to persevere and flourish as a leader is not easy. On pages 95–97, I explore how to deal with imposter syndrome, a common phenomenon that many leaders face, but for now, my recommended approach to help you to start building your confidence is to:

Forget what came before
You are a leader now. Your path here is irrelevant, and whatever role or roles you had which got you here are not the role you are performing now.

Recognise your journey
Being a leader doesn't usually happen overnight. You will have taken steps up and sideways as you progressed towards this point. Owning your leadership journey and being able to tell others how you got here will give you confidence that you have earned the right to be in the role.

Learn, read and listen
There is so much out there on leadership – get involved! What works for others? What blogs or podcasts can you follow where you get to hear from inspirational leaders about their challenges and how they have gained their confidence? Steven Bartlett's *Diary of a CEO* podcast is a great source of inspiration. Consider reading some leadership books to build your knowledge. I provide examples scattered throughout this book which might help start your list, but please ask others what has inspired them. The more you learn, the more you can apply.

Engage in formal learning
This could be anything from a study on an area of leadership to a master's in a specialised discipline or a general management qualification. You may also be fortunate enough to do an MBA, which I found hugely useful and is a generalist overview across many disciplines in managing businesses.

Know that repetition leads to confidence
Intentional repetition and dedicated practice will help lead to greater levels of skill and competence. This is a continuous improvement process, as you don't do something once and just 'get it'. You need to keep learning and growing and continuing to build competence, which will lead to greater confidence. As American philosopher Will Durant said, paraphrasing Aristotle, 'We are what we repeatedly do. Excellence, then, is not an act but a habit.'

Be OK with failure
Not just that: tell others that failing is part of a learning journey and is allowed! Failing fast and learning is a great way to see what works and what doesn't. Having the confidence to be a risk taker and learning how to take calculated risks is important for team and organisational development.

Have allies as well as challengers
Consider who your allies are – those who can give you input when you ask and provide support. They are helpful colleagues to have, but ensure they are not seen as favourites. Ensure to also engage with those who provide healthy constructive criticism or think differently to you as they can help you test new ideas and proposals.

> Embrace self-assurance – take ownership of your skills, abilities and decisions as this can help you take purposeful action and push the boundaries for growing the organisation that you are a part of. Being able to lead with confidence provides a feeling of trust and demonstrates you are focused on making responsible decisions for the business and have the team's best interests at the forefront.
> *Amanda Foreshaw, HR lead, strategic business partner and leadership coach*

I recommend *The Confidence Code* (2014) by Katty Kay and Claire Shipman, which is a practical guide to help you with understanding the importance of this essential belief. It addresses how to achieve confidence for women at all stages of their careers.

Finding the right coach, mentor or champion

As you prepare for your leadership role, you may need a bit of help. This could come in the form of a mentor, a coach or a champion. There are differences between these three types of supporters.

Coach

The idea of a coach is to have someone in your professional corner who, over time, will get to know you well, understand your needs and can help to create strategies for you to achieve your professional goals. Sessions feel like a personal self-discovery voyage, aided by expertly asked questions that help you to find answers within yourself.

Mentor

A mentor will be more directive than a coach. They might use their own personal experience to guide the discussion and learning. Mentors also offer advice and input to your thinking. They may engage you in informal learning through helping you to build your personal and professional skills and abilities. Mentors help mentees to become more effective members of an organisation.

Champion

Also known as an advocate or an ambassador, this is a far less formal arrangement, as you don't necessarily ask people to *champion you*. However, if you can find one or more champions, they can be very useful allies and may open doors for you. Aim to provide value to this person in return for their endorsement and support. One technique for building a mutually respectful relationship is to ask interesting and thought-provoking questions, which allow you to learn and the champion to share their wisdom.

Finding your professional support

A good first step is to see if your organisation has a scheme for identifying and providing a coach or mentor. This could be an internal colleague or sourced via external support.

It might be that you need to find your own coach, mentor or champion. Before you start drawing up a wish list, it is important to be clear about what your goals are, especially when it comes to professional coaching. Goals should ideally be measurable and specific.

?

→ What **coaching goals** do you have?
→ Are these linked to common challenges such as dealing with difficult situations or tackling conflict?
→ Might you have a technical area deficiency (for example, finance) where a coach might help you identify strategies to seek clarity and gain greater understanding?
→ Maybe you are a leader who is not good at delegation and finds it hard to trust others with tasks?
→ Perhaps you simply lack confidence, as many leaders do, and could use assistance with this element?

?

→ What **mentoring goals** might you have?
→ What are the areas you most want to work on?
→ Are there issues you would like to address for your personal career development?
→ Can you identify an area of development that you wish to work on and then find someone who has excelled in this and might share their practical tips and techniques?

Common goals may include building better connections, advancing leadership skills, improving communication or achieving better work–life balance.

?

→ What **ambassadorial support** might you need from a **champion**?
→ Are you relatively new to a sector and need someone to open doors for you or act as an advocate so you

are well positioned to be invited to engage in key networks or groups?

A goal here might be to build the right relationships, to gain access to the best decision-making or thought leadership forums, or to be in the right rooms so you can be a representative for your organisation – all of which may only be possible by being introduced by the right person with the relevant connections.

Once you are clear about your goals, you are ready to find the right person to support you. Support from a mentor will draw on their lived and professional experience. And, if their background has relevancy to you, all they need to support you effectively is sufficient understanding of the mentoring process. Coaching, in contrast, usually requires more formalised training and development to be effective.

If you are looking for a mentor, one option is to consider whether you have a networked path to the right person: someone who specialises in areas that you specifically want to address. Using tools such as LinkedIn and other networking sites can provide a potential shortlist. If you work back from their connections to yours, can you find a chain? If so, it is possible to build on introductions until you reach your desired contact (as long as the chain is relatively short!). You may also wish to approach them directly and ask politely if they have time and space to act as a mentor to a willing mentee.

Finding a coach is slightly different. Aside from using your network, there are coaching websites such as the International Coaching Federation, whose Credentialed Coach Finder (CCF) is a free searchable directory with listings for thousands of qualified ICF-credentialed coaches worldwide.

Finding and building a relationship with a career champion is a more subtle and nuanced task, so I have given you an idea here about how to introduce yourself to get the ball rolling.

> **⚒ Toolkit item 7:**
> **Introducing yourself to a champion**
>
> You may get a chance to introduce yourself to a career **champion** in person (see insights about the art of networking on page 109). If not, my approach has been to email or use a networking site direct messenger to say who I am, what I have found particularly interesting about their passion for X, Y or Z and then ask whether, time permitting, it would be possible to meet them and buy them a coffee so I might get a chance to understand more and hear their insights and thoughts. It is worth also acknowledging that their time is precious, so you would also be grateful for just a brief call or video meeting.
>
> This often works, as individuals can be generous with their time and enjoy sharing their thoughts and passion on topics where they have expertise.

Some positives and health warnings

There are many positives to finding support. New leadership roles can be a bit lonely and sometimes daunting. Even if this is not the case for you, you may wish to find someone out there to provide guidance, support and/or to be a sounding board to test your thinking or someone who will ask you good questions to help you find clarity. Many leaders seek help, so don't let ego or uncertainty get in the way of enlisting support. I have benefited from many coaches and mentors over time, and one standout (Pete Ashby) was instrumental in boosting me when I needed it most. You are not always lucky to find the perfect fit on the first go; don't be put off, and keep searching till you meet someone who will be both your cheerleader and your critical friend.

Despite their benefits, there may come a time when a relationship with a coach, mentor or champion will come to an end. In some circumstances, there is a natural end to the engagement and the need has been addressed. However, there are also times when a more difficult dynamic can occur. You may no longer find their expertise as relevant to you as you develop your capabilities, you might feel that the questions you are being asked are not challenging your thinking, or there may be a professional conflict that makes the arrangement unviable. This is a difficult experience and can be emotional if you have established a good bond. If you need to conclude matters, being clear, polite and kind is best. If the decision is not yours, do not take it personally. There will be many others who will willingly support you throughout your career. For further assistance, see the guidance in Chapter 4 on how to have challenging conversations (page 114).

Getting the right sponsor I think is key as is recognising and aligning with genuine leaders and managers.
Faye Cannings, regeneration lead practitioner, local government

Every new leader should have a mentor or coach. They help build confidence, job satisfaction and offer support. For me it was great knowing a skilled professional was there for me no matter what happened!
Dr Catherine Manning, PhD in mentoring

Chapter reflections

You should now feel even more ready for your role than you were when you started this book. You ought to be able to describe your leadership style, you will hopefully feel set up for your first day on the job, and if you have already commenced your role before reading this, I hope there have still been insights that you will apply in your first few weeks and months. For example, do you have a mentor, coach or champion? If not, it's not too late to find one!

You are as prepared as you can be. Now I want to help you through those first few weeks and months, starting with putting leadership into practice in your new role.

2 Leadership in practice

After taking those initial steps that should help to set you up as a leader, it is time to turn to applying your leadership in practice.

As a leader, you will likely have a team, although not all do. Some operate in a standalone role where they work with others through a matrix structure. As that role is less usual for a first-time leader, I will concentrate here on supporting you as someone who is establishing a relationship with a new team reporting to you. I was mostly guided by instincts when I led my first small team of colleagues in Liverpool, in the north of England. However, it was in those early days that I started noting what did and didn't work for teams to operate well, and over the years I have had a chance to refine this and finesse it to share with you in this chapter.

Establishing the operating framework for an effective team

There are many books, and a lot of theory, on how to manage a team well, such as Stephen Robbins' *The Truth About Managing People* (2002). This is a well-studied discipline, so I won't go into the basics. Instead, I will focus on the operating conditions for successful team working.

The size of the team and nature of engagement (in person, remote, hybrid) does make a difference in terms of the logistics. However, I have come to conclude that whatever the circumstances, there are still essential ways in which teams should operate for success, and some clear dos and don'ts.

Operating as a successful team

What does a team need to be successful? My recommendations are as follows.

1. A team needs a leader

Someone to set the tone, the direction, frame the discussion, provide the parameters, take final decisions, facilitate discussion, be an enabler of others and do so much more.

Teams without a clear leader, or that lack effective leadership, are generally less productive, failing to move towards the delivery of a clear vision. That's not to say that there aren't some self-managed or self-organised teams that work. These are becoming increasingly common in some workplaces, especially in the technology sector. For those operating in these teams, effective team working must be heightened, as decisions are generally open for discussion, with input given from many sources, and agreement needs to be reached on a range of ways of working, including accountability, delegation and decision making. Thus far, I haven't come across many teams or organisations that have sufficient experience or the interpersonal skills needed for this to work brilliantly. Hence, most teams need a leader.

2. A team needs to work effectively together

Ongoing clashes and disruption ultimately stall progress and can be barriers to effective working relationships. However, it is important to air tensions and find safe spaces to facilitate discussions that raise and address issues. Healthy tensions can spark debate, creativity and fresh thinking, but they need to be well handled. Effective team working requires staff to set aside personal prejudices to be able to collaborate successfully. An effective team is one that learns together and aims to improve its collective performance.

A team works effectively with a leader.

3. A team needs to know how it interfaces with other teams
Too often, teams can operate in isolation from other teams (known as silo working). There may be factors that cause this, such as staff geographical spread, team characteristics or the behaviour of the team leader. It might be that the team has a long-established history in the organisation but hasn't considered how company developments and new teams have changed operating dynamics. Or it could be that a recently introduced team is yet to understand how it interacts with others. Further distancing can be caused when organisational structures change following mergers and acquisitions, or when a service is taken over from another organisation and the staff transfer with the service delivery (known legally as TUPE when this is under their previous terms and conditions).

A team may need to have a relationship with every other team in the organisation, but they might not see that. Fully exploring with your team how they should interact with other teams can be a helpful exercise. This may not necessarily be about interacting to get work done. It may be that teams simply need to share intelligence or pre-warn others of upcoming projects or activities that might have consequences for other departments.

With some teams, there may be established protocols for engagement and minimum response times, such as when IT teams address issues. With others, there may be fewer formal arrangements and it's up to individuals across the business to play their part in being collaborative and engaging with others.

The team leader also needs to check that these engagements are happening.

An effective team is a well-connected team.

4. A team must operate with transparency, respect and trust
This is essential for a well-functioning team, as being transparent, showing respect for each other and for each other's time, is key to building trust.

Creating an environment of trust in a team is not always easy. However, there are options. Trust can come from personal connections, which can be formed through showing vulnerability. An ex-colleague of mine came up with the great idea of regularly (weekly or fortnightly) starting team meetings with a random question colleagues can choose to answer, which shares an insight into who they are. Questions you could use include:

→ What was your favourite TV programme, book or magazine as a child?
→ If you could choose one meal to repeat at least weekly, what would it be?
→ What is your dream holiday destination?

A well-connected team leads to openness and transparency.

5. A team needs to demonstrate consensus when exiting a conversation
It is highly unlikely that you'll achieve genuine consensus on a challenging work matter. However, the place to thrash this out is among the team you're working in. Once that team sets a direction, facilitated by their leader, then, if all objections have been raised, heard and addressed, a team must exit the conversation prepared to demonstrate consensus beyond the discussion.

There are few things more frustrating for a leader than thinking that the team has agreed a path, particularly if setting

Leadership in practice

the direction has been challenging, to find one or more team members criticising the action, however privately this has been done. It is undermining, breaks trust and causes unnecessary tension. As a leader, you will need to challenge this behaviour, but also address the situation individually with the relevant parties while reiterating the operating protocols for effective team engagement to the wider group.

A team that operates with trust will have greater confidence that the group will support the consensus reached.

> *Toolkit item 8:*
> *Managing a team on a contentious matter*
>
> It is not always easy dealing with sensitive or contentious matters as a team. As a leader, you could handle this by:
>
> → Explaining that you want to debate the topic to hear the full range of views.
> → Being clear that your role as leader is to be aided in decision making by listening to all perspectives and gaining greater clarity and insight from the diversity of thought.
> → Considering whether it is appropriate to be guided by a majority vote to set the direction. If a debate proves to be too fractious, this may not be the right course of action. Note that it is important to be mindful of decision quality versus acceptance. See the section on 'Making decisions' on page 76.
> → Being clear about how the decision will be made. Will you give your team a chance to share their views but ultimately decide, or will you put it to a vote and go with the majority? If you are clear from the start on this, colleagues will be more prepared to accept the fact that the outcome may not go their way and will at least feel that their opinions have been heard.

6. A team needs to live the company values

Demonstrating and living company values and not just seeing them as a set of words that sit on a poster on the wall is a useful way to guide both team and whole company behaviour.

If a team is struggling to demonstrate the values, there may be something wrong, which is worth exploring. If the values feel truly *fit for purpose*, then they are a great way to both deliver high performance as a team and highlight when any actions or behaviours undermine the agreed way of operating.

If the team is the executive (top) team and is failing to demonstrate these values, this could lead to distrust and frustration from other employees, which in turn can have a negative impact on morale.

A team that demonstrates consensus, including on how it lives the company values, will garner greater respect from staff.

7. A team needs to understand how it contributes to organisational strategy

It is important as a team leader to ensure that your team appreciates that every area of the company has a role to play in ensuring its success. This is especially necessary with some support functions, as it isn't always obvious to staff how they might contribute to the fulfilment of strategic objectives. Drawing a connection between the team and the role that it plays in delivering on the organisational plan is important for the psychological contract between an employee and the organisation.

A team which aligns its work with strategy generates a closer psychological contract between employees and the organisation.

8. A team needs difference

Diversity is essential if a team is going to avoid creating products or services that would only be appropriate for themselves or people with the same experience. We should seek to understand one another's differences, even if this leads to some discomfort as we grapple to get it right, as doing so will lead to greater comprehension, learning and conversation, which enables richer insights.

Understanding how your team is operating is essential for effective leadership. There are many tools available to test the composition of a team, such as Myers–Briggs or Belbin. These can help you get a sense of the configuration of a team, the leadership styles present and personal preferences on how team members like to engage. For example, some of these assessments (like Myers–Briggs) can help to identify if someone feels that they are more extroverted or introverted.

A team needs difference to operate in the most effective way.

If there is a missing characteristic or skill in a team, it might be that you need to intentionally seek that input through additional contributions or expertise. However, if you don't have the luxury of adding more resource to your team to provide that missing input, you can find creative ways to get the team you currently have to operate in a way that brings in the missing perspectives.

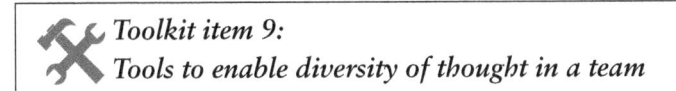

> *Toolkit item 9:*
> *Tools to enable diversity of thought in a team*
>
> A useful tool is Edward de Bono's *Six Thinking Hats* (1985), which can help you to ensure that you use lateral thinking to evaluate a proposition. The idea is that members of the team wear an invisible hat, with the intention of operating in the mode of that hat colour throughout a conversation, until they are asked to switch to a new hat and way of thinking. Having all the hats represented means that you have a variety of different perspectives on a problem. The hats are:

> → Blue: 'Conductor's Hat' – you control thinking and manage decision making.
> → Green: 'Creative Hat' – you explore a range of ideas and possibilities.
> → Red: 'Hat for the Heart' – you lead on representing feelings and go with gut instinct.
> → Yellow: 'Optimist's Hat' – you consider issues in the most positive way.
> → Black: 'Judge's Hat' – you are cautious, even pessimistic. You explain concerns and critique options.
> → White: 'Factual Hat' – you are the check and balance on what is missing.

Dos and don'ts for operating an effective team

I have come to learn some essential considerations which I like to apply to ensure successful team operations.

Do:

→ celebrate successes when teams have worked effectively together – it is good to reinforce what has worked well
→ assess issues when things haven't worked and ask yourself and your team 'why?'
→ apply a lessons-learnt discipline to see how you can improve
→ use team assessment tools or frameworks to understand how balanced the team is
→ recognise that cultural setting is a key factor in how teams operate and, in some cultures, greater understanding of cultural intelligence and context is required. For example, hierarchy can have an impact on decision making and reaching consensus.

Don't:

→ worry if you can't achieve all of this – it takes time for teams to form and bond and get to the levels of trust needed for true empathy, cooperation and collaboration
→ see these as the only criteria for effective team working – there are lots of other ideas out there.

This next advice brings out some many important points for this book, not just on what it takes to build confidence as a leader, but also on the importance of having a wide range of views and expertise to achieve success:

I am a senior leader within the NHS leading a team of just over 300, the majority of them technical experts. Earlier on in my career I thought I needed to have all the answers and my credibility would depend on my technical skills alone. I have since realised that it is all my leadership skills that are far more important and they have a far greater impact on the team, and in turn, on delivery. I am a big advocate of compassionate leadership and a believer in championing and empowering each other. We don't always get it right, particularly when busy, but it is through bringing together our broad range of skills, expertise and perspectives, moving away from our silos, forging positive relationships and supporting each other that we can achieve so much more.

One of my favourite quotes is from [former prime minister of New Zealand] Jacinda Ardern:

'One of the criticisms I've faced over the years is that I am not aggressive enough or assertive enough, or maybe somehow because I am empathetic, it means I'm weak. I totally rebel against that. I refuse to believe that you cannot be both compassionate and strong.'

It rings true in so many ways and I encourage you to reflect on the examples you've seen, or set, when it comes to compassionate leadership.
Sarah Stevens, deputy director, National Disease Registration Service

Leading your first major initiative

My first major initiative was a project to create an operating manual for the whole organisation. It felt like an overwhelming and significant piece of work and it took me some time to break it down and plan out what I needed to do. I knew it involved the entire company and would be high profile. I knew it would mean coordinating leaders who were senior to me. I also knew it would take many months (in the end it was nine), and I understood that I had overall accountability for this work. I did manage to develop my own successful methodology to undertake this work, but I know it would have been useful if I'd had access to a guiding framework: a way to consider aspects such as the project value, importance, implications and approach. This would have helped not only in my planning but in being able to articulate the project's complexity and significance to others.

As a leader, it's likely that you will lead a major initiative, and this could happen early in your new role. This could be a new project, like mine, but you might also inherit a piece of work that is already in development. It could be a cross-organisational project or only involve your team. It could be a project that requires a substantial financial investment and/or have a bearing on the achievement of an important company objective.

Having now worked on multiple initiatives, I have developed a toolkit of questions and methods that I'm sharing here. My aim is to give you a framework so you can approach your own first initiative with confidence.

However, I won't cover the main project management principles here, as this is a book for leaders, not managers. If you're interested in learning more about effective project management, there are plenty of resources available, such as Jack Meredith and Samuel Mantel Jr's *Project Management* (2011). To enhance your knowledge, you could also study project management, with options ranging from courses that provide a basic grounding through to more complex overviews such as a PRINCE2 qualification.

Starting a new initiative

My first Toolkit item for leading a major initiative provides a list of essential exploratory questions that you can use to identify whether you need to undertake further review or action. Ideally, you'll have some project management resource to track and monitor the responses to these questions and act accordingly. The elements that follow will then help you to understand who your stakeholders are, identify roles and responsibilities, define your own leadership role, work out how issues that may arise will be addressed, assess the viability and direction you might need to take with an already established project and write up your findings in a clear and compelling way.

Toolkit item 10:
Exploratory questions for a new initiative

As a leader of an initiative, you will want to understand the following:

→ Is this a strategic project, an operational one or both?
→ Will this project need input from individuals or companies outside yours?
→ Does this project require financial investment and has a budget already been agreed?

→ What type of project management approach needs to be applied? Is this an agile project, where the project is broken into stages (sprints) and components are delivered and evaluated throughout the project? Or is it one that is more traditional, with activities that will happen in consecutive order and delivery assessed at the end?
→ Are there any major dependencies – links between one or more aspects of the project which are reliant on one another for success?
→ What are the intended benefits of the project?
→ Are there any reasons why this project is not viable or feasible? Do studies need to be undertaken to determine that?
→ Can this project be led by you and/or (some of) your team, or might it require cross-organisational working groups?
→ What roles will people need to take on the project?
→ What other work will be happening at the same time?
→ Who are the key stakeholders?
→ Are you happy to be the senior responsible officer on the project and public (internal or external) face of the project? Are you the right person to lead this work?
→ Do you have a team you wish to bring together for this project? When assembling the project team, take account of the 'Operating as a successful team' guidance on page 48.

Answering these questions is part of the information-gathering and planning stage before you commence the work.

A key criterion for any work, not just for an initiative, is to understand each other's respective roles and responsibilities. I have found that a great way to tackle this is to use a responsibility assignment model, such as RACI.

Leadership in practice

> **Toolkit item 11:
> The RACI model**
>
> Using a RACI model is a useful way to work out who the key stakeholders for any initiative are. In short, the letters stand for:
>
> R – Responsible: a manager or team member who is directly responsible for successfully completing a project task.
>
> A – Accountable: the person with final authority over the successful completion of the specific task or deliverable.
>
> C – Consult: someone with unique insights the team will consult, or, in a more nuanced way, individuals or companies which need to be consulted as part of ensuring project success.
>
> I – Inform: the key stakeholders (internal and external) who aren't directly involved but should be kept up to speed.

Use this framework to put names against each RACI element for each key milestone to help you with the effective leadership of the initiative.

Your leadership role on the project

As a leader, you will also need to think about your own role in this piece of work, and the form of leadership it might require. You'll need to be clear about the risks and issues associated with the project and how the project contributes to the organisation's strategic goals, so you can meaningfully update the relevant 'inform' stakeholders at the right points and in the relevant way. Think about the approach you will take to leading this work and answer these reflection questions:

?

- → What leadership style might the situation require?
- → How will you ensure you are credible when you talk about this – particularly if it's a technical piece of work beyond your area of expertise?
- → How can you ensure you have a clearly articulated description of the initiative?
- → How will you enthuse and excite others?
- → Do you need to do an official launch?
- → How will you celebrate successes along the way?
- → Will you step in if issues arise which may impact on the successful completion of the work?

Further to *how* you will lead, you will need to think about the project decisions you'll need to make as a leader:

- → Will you want or need to fix or address issues which arise, and if so, do you have the skills and expertise to do so?
- → How will you update the relevant parties that you need to 'inform' about the work?
- → How will you ensure that the balance is right between time, cost and quality?
- → Are there quick wins that you'll be able to share with staff?
- → Does your work have an impact elsewhere in the organisation and if so, how will you engage those people?
- → Once the work is complete, how will you mark the occasion – will you celebrate success?

A key tip for leading an initiative: as the project concludes, it's always worth doing a lessons-learnt exercise – using a framework to critically evaluate what worked and what didn't and what you would do differently in the future.

Inheriting an already established piece of work

It can be slightly easier to kick off an initiative and have full accountability from the beginning than to inherit a project. The early exploratory questions you need to ask in this case are somewhat different. For example:

→ What stage is this project at?
→ Are there any known risk and issues recorded on a RAID (risks, actions, issues and decisions) log?
→ Why have you inherited this work? Was this led by your predecessor or handed over to you from someone else in the organisation?
→ What is the current progress of the project? Is it on track?
→ What is the external perception of the project? What do key stakeholders think?
→ Are the executive or the governing body/board aware of any issues? If so, will there be a requirement to update them at some stage?
→ Are the benefits realistic and/or are the intended completion timeframes viable?
→ How is the morale of the project team?
→ What is the perception of the wider business of this work?

A tip for this stage of exploration: as you seek out answers to the questions above, be wary of criticising work underway as this could be a bad start for you and your team. Make sure you gather both qualitative (feedback) and quantitative (data) evidence and don't form conclusions based on limited sources of intelligence.

Depending on the outcome of the investigations you have undertaken, there may be several outcomes:

All may be fine. You may just need to use the established monitoring framework in place and, assuming there are no issues. Your role is to caretake the project through to completion.

There are small issues or tweaks you need to address. You can put in place plans or actions to resolve these problems.

There are some more fundamental issues that need looking at. Consider who you need to update regarding your exploratory review. This is especially relevant if you need to change a parameter on the classic project management triangle, which reflects the challenge of the combined constraints of time, quality and cost. For example, you may need to ask for more time, adjust the quality or scope of the output that can be expected, and/or require a change in budget. If a change to any of those constraints occurs, you'll need to think about what that means for the other elements.

There needs to be a full revision. In this case, you'll need to lead a turnaround of the project, assuming the conclusion is that it's essential to still deliver the desired benefit and output/outcomes of the work. This could involve stopping to reassess what can be achieved, which may lead to resetting the objectives and associated outcomes and then creating a fresh plan to deliver against new parameters.

You might conclude that it's not possible to turn the project around, or that the reason for doing this project is no longer justified or relevant. You'll then need to propose that the work should cease entirely.

Aside from the first option, the remainder require diplomacy, possibly difficult conversations and handling with care. If you aren't sure and have a support mechanism in place such as a coach, you might want to talk to them about this confidentially. It is generally sensible to talk to a line manager about your findings.

> **⚒ Toolkit item 12: Producing written findings following project assessments**
>
> When presenting findings from an assessment on how any project is delivering, it is wise to produce a written update. You might like to use a framework such as the one below:
>
> 1. Present an executive summary that details the issue at a high level and provides high-level recommendations.
> 2. Set out what methodology you have used to complete this assessment to draw your conclusions.
> 3. Set out the detailed findings.
> 4. Present detailed recommendations based on those findings.
> 5. Share your data sources and intelligence gathering in the form of annexes. (Be careful of confidentiality. It might be that you need to anonymise some of the sources of your insights.)

Leading a working group on a sensitive topic

Many companies nowadays intentionally tackle complex and sensitive subjects by appointing roles to lead on these areas or by putting in place internal forums, and you might end up leading one of these groups. In my experience, these have included initiatives covering diversity, anti-racism, equity, inclusion and belonging, mental health and wellbeing. There are many other key themes which organisations choose to address.

If you're asked to lead a group, there are a few considerations I wanted to share:

→ It's OK not to be an expert on all or any of these areas. Indeed, it would be wrong to suggest that you are,

especially if you have no lived experience. The nature and sensitivity of these topics means that you can lose credibility and, worst case, cause offence if you get it wrong, especially as these themes are of high importance and value to employees.
→ There might already be a framework established for these working groups which can guide your approach, such as a terms of reference (ToR).
→ If not, and you're starting a group from scratch, then it's worth establishing a clear set of deliverables for the group through a ToR, setting out the purpose of the group, what topics it's expecting to cover and what it should not, and what decision-making responsibility (if any) the group has.
→ There is significant value in well-managed and facilitated conversation and discussion to explore topics and gain greater understanding. To do this, you need to try and establish a safe space and psychological safety for the group so that openness, inclusivity and confidentiality (if necessary) can be features of your discussion.
→ It's sensible, where possible, to get external input and assistance to check you're addressing the right subjects, to see if your policies and procedures are appropriate and to demonstrate your commitment to getting this right, rather than it being perceived as a token effort.
→ One essential piece of advice is to not look to those with the relevant protected characteristics to 'solve' the problem, be a spokesperson or to be expected to educate others. This is likely to cause offence and is not appropriate.
→ Form an action plan that you share openly with staff. This will help to demonstrate commitment to the topic of the working group. Once done, it's important to remember to update colleagues on your progress.

Leadership in practice

Dealing with your first board or departmental meeting

At some point, you will attend a meeting with senior internal managers and/or external sponsors or shareholders. It might be that you're invited to present on the major initiative you are leading. Whatever the circumstances, you will want to be well prepared.

Preparation

Before your first meeting, especially a significant departmental, divisional or board meeting, it's a wise move to find out more about your organisation's governance structure. Companies have a range of different structures: some have trustees, some have directors, some have elected officials and potentially a range of other roles.

> *Toolkit item 13: Finding out about your organisation's approach to governance*
>
> 1. Look back at prior minutes and actions to get a sense of the discussion topics, the level of detail of the discussions, the nature of the information provided and what actions resulted.
> 2. If appropriate, ask to meet with the person who manages governance to find out more. This might be a director of governance or a company secretary – your HR colleagues should know who this is.
> 3. Companies produce financial statements and accounts that give overviews from governing bodies and are useful to read through if you are to attend a board meeting.
> 4. Organisations may also operate within certain requirements, such as the Charity Governance Code, which would be worth you understanding.

> 5. You might also research the backgrounds of the key stakeholders attending the meeting, especially the chair of the board, to gain clarity on how they operate. I worked at a company where the chair had written a book about the public sector, and a number of us found it useful to read to understand more about how they viewed the work we were doing.

You will need to think about what role you'll play in the meeting. You might be there to observe or not really be expected to contribute unless you're comfortable to. However, you may be there to play a more active part, such as being ready to respond to queries about the area you lead or to present an update on an initiative you're running. The key is to find out what's expected of you from your line manager so you can prepare thoroughly.

During the meeting

Listening is extremely important. You will undoubtedly have a lot to learn, and this will be a good opportunity to enhance your understanding. It will also help you identify any points where you can contribute.

Be observant as to how people interact with one another. Some meetings can be rather formal, with people respectfully waiting their turn to come in, whereas in some places the discussion flows more naturally. In some workplaces, it's practice to refer to meeting attendees by their formal roles, such as the chair of the meeting as 'the chair', whereas other leaders prefer to be referred to by their name.

Important meetings such as a divisional or board meeting are in place so that those with responsibility for governance oversight can fulfil their duty to critically assess the organisation and its leadership, and to provide insights and feedback given their relevant areas of expertise.

For those answerable for the work (the employees), there's a delicate balance to be achieved between giving the assurance needed that all is well and making sure that you're not seen as trying to hide any flaws. It's also important to be open to hearing the views of the governing body representatives. My advice is to err on the side of being thankful for input and to be respectful and open minded. There's a lot you can learn and improve upon given feedback from these meetings. The key is to not be defensive in your responses to questions and queries.

Although these meetings can be a little daunting, you're not expected to give lots of input straight away.

> Don't feel you need to add value immediately – it's fine to observe and ask questions to clarify the situation at the first meeting. This is particularly the case if you are moving into a new sector or area of work; to contribute meaningfully you will need time to understand the situation, organisational history and board dynamics. You have been hired for your skills and experience; this will be realised over time and the board will recognise this, so take the pressure off yourself for the first meeting. It may be helpful to be explicit about this, stating informally to the chair or to the full board or team you will mainly be observing the first meeting and will contribute to future meetings. The board or department team members are likely to appreciate your openness.
> *Susan Hamilton, hospice CEO and non-executive director in housing and health*

Dealing with key external stakeholders

Stakeholder groupings
Many leadership roles have a requirement to engage with external stakeholders.

Stakeholders fall into many categories. These include beneficiaries such as communities or customers, funders such as owners who supply capital or equity and have a say in how things are run, or private finance and investors who have a right to accurate and timely information about the organisation's performance, or providers of public funding such as contracts or grants, where rigour is expected on how funding is spent. Other stakeholders include operational partners such as suppliers or delivery organisations, your staff and board members, and technical or specialist stakeholders such as government agencies, media and PR agencies or trade unions. As these stakeholders are either fairly operational or dealt with by technical specialists (for example, trade unions by HR colleagues), I'm only going to focus in detail on strategic stakeholders, with whom I imagine you will have your main interface.

Working with strategic stakeholders
A strategic stakeholder is a partner who can enhance your strategy in a range of ways. Ideally, this is a mutually beneficial relationship that may gain from information and intelligence sharing, advocacy for each other's missions, opening doors to influencers, peer support and review.

Choosing strategic partners carefully is important. These partners have a significant chance of acting as an enabler to your organisation; however, if you get this wrong, they may also harm your company (for example, by aligning with other partners who could damage your brand).

If you're in the process of establishing a new strategic

partnership, undertaking research before you initiate contact can help to avoid some of the possible challenges that could arise from picking the wrong partner. Keeping this research current is also important.

Five essential details to understand about a strategic partner include:

1. Their business plan and strategy.
2. Their mission and vision.
3. What they advocate for or stand for.
4. If they have experienced any controversy in the recent past and whether issues are resolved.
5. Who their leader is and what that person cares about.

You can find much of this from company websites, financial statements and accounts and social media searches.

A challenge with managing these relationships is that not every organisation properly tracks who their strategic partners are. This is because the relationship is less transactional and is more informal. I would recommend having a strategic stakeholder map for your area of work or the organisation overall. This should:

→ reflect the partner's positioning resulting from a scored assessment of the influence you perceive that they hold as well as their interest in your organisation
→ use the output of this assessment to lead to a prioritisation plan that uses a ranking to place those you most wish to engage with at the top of your focus list alongside the desired next steps on engagement with that partner
→ align with a tracker that records the latest answers to the five areas above that you would be wise to understand about that organisation so that if something changes – for example, the leader of that company is replaced – you are prompted to reassess the positioning of that partner on your map.

It's worth noting that these relationships develop through building trust and gaining each other's confidence over time.

Ways in which you might support one another
To think about the value you might gain from a strategic partner, my table below contains some of the areas of potential mutual benefit for this relationship.

Area	Purpose
Rich data and insights	The more data you have access to, the better informed you will be (as long as you make good use of it and the data is clean). This can help situate your understanding in a wider context. There may be protocols and restrictions on sharing data, so you will need to check.
Common customers	You and another partner may have customers or consumers in common and you might be able to enhance your offer or service through collaboration.
Sector intelligence	Aside from data and research, there are other forms of intelligence you might be able to share. Some of this might be anecdotal and you can use your respective relationships to test theories about what you have heard. You might also want to discuss the latest trends in your work and identify other partners you might individually or both want to engage with.
Mission overlap	When you have mission overlap, there should be lots of opportunity for collaboration. However, there may be some elements you want to keep confidential, particularly if the partner might also be a competitor now or in the future. One of the ways in which you might collaborate is to publicly support one another on important topics. This might be in the form of supporting public debates or advocacy efforts.

Leadership in practice

Useful connections	It's likely that partners will have contacts you do not have. You might introduce one another to a potential collaborator, or a partner might be able to get you involved with work that would be of great benefit for your organisation. For example, if a partner was on a committee or a thought leadership group that would be helpful for your work.
Peer support and review	It can be lonely in leadership roles! Sometimes having a peer-level individual with whom you can confidentially engage and talk through challenges and successes is highly beneficial. Just be conscious that there needs to be a high level of trust in place for this to work and you'll need to understand your respective motivations clearly. You should never share anything that's confidential to your company.

?

Having read through this section, do you know who the strategic partners might be for your work? Do you have robust stakeholder mapping?

Toolkit item 14:
Effective strategic partnership working

It's useful to remember that you have no obligation to be in a strategic relationship and neither does the partner. With that in mind:

1. Celebrate any success you mutually deliver/achieve.
2. Test the benefit that they perceive is generated by your relationship.
3. Check there is continued value in you engaging in this partnership.
→ If circumstances change, assess whether the relationship is still appropriate (for example, if you're competing for the same work).

Effective communication

As a leader, you're expected to have high standards of communication, so while I'm assuming that by this point you have mastered effective (and concise) emails and impactful presentations, I'm going to share some hints and tips on leadership-focused communications that might be less familiar to you.

Written reports

Your company may have an in-house style or template. If not, I find that, as a minimum, you would be best to include:

1. A strategic executive summary that sets out the purpose of the report, the intended audience, the high-level findings and key recommendations.
2. The methodology you used to produce the report findings.
3. The detailed findings (this may include graphs or data as well as narrative analysis).
4. The full recommendations based on those detailed findings (depending on what your report is intended to do). I've found that with external stakeholders, and particularly directors or boards, it's helpful to present options where you can, alongside your recommendation on which you judge is the best one to proceed with.
5. Share your data sources and intelligence gathering in the form of annexes. (Remember to be careful of confidentiality.)

Essential tips to help you consider how best to frame this report:

Who is this for?

→ Before you get started, make sure you're clear on who the report is being written for, as this will help you to set the tone, use the right language and consider if the audience will easily understand the subject matter or whether you'll need to provide a greater level of explanation for context.

What is it intended to achieve?

→ Consider what the report is aiming to achieve. Is it aiming to persuade others on a direction, provide a briefing or recommend a course of action to the reader? It's important to do the necessary research to gather all the essential intelligence for your report.

Video messages

These are useful when undertaking staff briefings and are a helpful way to ensure that everyone gets the same message delivered in a consistent way. It's worth at least one rehearsal before you deliver the message and keeping what you're saying to high-level bullets, so you don't look as if you're reading a lot of text, but instead can look into the camera and engage directly with your audience.

In-person speeches

Many leaders find standing up and giving speeches difficult; however, it is a critical part of your remit. That's why there are several courses out there to help. I would recommend Toastmasters courses, which help with not just prepared speeches but spontaneous speaking too, which is useful, as is practising regularly to build skills and get rid of nerves. One way to get better is to just keep doing it – you will improve over time! Even some of the most well-known international leaders will admit they sometimes get nervous. I have found the following techniques useful:

→ Know your presentation inside out. That doesn't mean over-rehearsing it, but being sure about what's going to appear on your next slide, or what you intend to say next, as this gives you a lot of reassurance and makes your delivery more natural.

→ Think in advance about how you want to deliver. Are you going to walk around or are you going to stand at a lectern? What will be available to you in the room? Checking out the space and venue first and making sure that whatever technology you're going to use is working will give you confidence.

→ To help quieten nerves, I use calming breathing techniques or visualisation exercises to relax before delivering a presentation.

→ Some people find it helpful to imagine themselves as an alter ego, perhaps someone who is slightly fiercer and with a braver personality. (Have you ever watched *The Mindy Project*? When Mindy has to deal with something difficult, she tells herself she isn't Mindy, but a warrior named 'Beyoncé Pad Thai'!)

→ Calming natural remedy drops or lozenges can also be useful. If you plan on taking these, try them in advance in case you don't like the taste.

→ Remember, no one wants you to fail. The whole room is interested to hear what you have to say and will be much more on side than you realise.

A business case

These often differ from a written report. Again, there may be a preferred in-house template. If not, I like to include the following sections:

1. An overview of the business case, the benefits and aims – essentially the reason why you're making this proposal.
2. The data and evidence that support the need you're trying to address.

Leadership in practice

3. The key objectives, scope and deliverables.
4. Who the main stakeholders are.
5. Financial information covering costs, return on investment, impact on cash flow, sensitivity analysis and any other relevant reporting.
6. A plan for how you would deliver, which might be a roadmap setting out the steps you will go through.
7. A summary matrix of risks and barriers, and how you intend to overcome them.

Try to keep this high level and, where necessary, add supporting detail in annexes. These can provide more information on your evidence base, the data you have used, who you consulted and how you built the business case.

Communicating is complex, but as Dionne describes, it may be simpler than you think:

> There is really only one measure of effective communication and that is whether your message has been understood by the people you are sharing it with.
>
> We can often spend a long time perfecting presentations, briefings, your approach to chairing meetings, appraisals, often forgetting that it's far less about how you perform and more about what they receive.
>
> Get to know your audience. Your team/audience/stakeholders etc are made up of a set of unique individuals and rarely does a single approach meet their diverse needs, and failing to accommodate all these needs can lead to limited progress and all-round frustration. Your audience will include reflectors, who will need time to consider the detail and risk; creators, who are constrained by detail and like to think or talk more about the opportunities and potential of ideas; those who are heavily driven to

minimising the impact on people; and those who just want a decision made. Work with your team – give time for the creative ideas to flow before creating more detailed documents for those who need to review. Consult where you can and be open to change, but when it's time to make a decision, do so with confidence. Don't try to please everyone.

Dionne Spence, chief officer, General Pharmaceutical Council

Making decisions

Leading on decision making

Fairly early on in your role, perhaps even on your first day, you will be required to make decisions. The nature of those decisions will vary. Some may be minor decisions and others may be major ones (with everything in between!). Examples could include:

Relatively minor	Making changes to how the team meets or interfaces with the organisation.
In between	Changing ways of working in your team for better efficiency or alignment.
Potentially major	Significant investment, choosing between two major initiatives that are both needed, restructuring your team.

With major decisions (and perhaps even some in-between ones), it's worth checking if you have the remit or authority to make those decisions on your own, or whether you would need sign-off or approval from a manager.

If you feel certain you're accountable for a decision, you may then wonder how to approach making it, and what input you might need from others. Decision making is one of the harder tasks that leaders face. There are lots of aspects you will need to consider. I find that the Vroom and Yetton decision-making model (Vroom and Jago 2007), which assesses decision quality against decision acceptance, is a helpful way to guide thinking. I have adapted and simplified the model here to share with you. It also addresses what decision-making style you might need to use.

The model takes three aspects into account:

1. **Decision quality** – the model asks you to think about how important it is for you to end up with the 'correct decision'. This may seem like an odd thing to consider, but what this means is that there are circumstances when some choices are more important than others. For example, organisations have finite resources so you can't apply intensive focus and lengthy reflection on every decision to get to the best outcome.
2. **Employee commitment** – employee buy-in could be material in some decisions. The level of interest employees might have will likely be linked to the extent to which the decision affects them.
3. **Time constraints** – how much time do you have? Sometimes you can't afford to wait and therefore need to make an instant decision. At other times you may have the luxury of a longer time period, allowing you to explore options and weigh up decision implications in detail.

> 🛠 **Toolkit item 15: The five Vroom and Yetton decision-making styles**
>
> I have adapted this model, which helps to frame five decision-making styles under three style headings.

Style	Detail
Autocratic style	1. You solve the problem or make the decision alone, using the information you have available to you.
	2. You get the information you need from staff but still make the decision alone. In gathering the information, you may or may not tell colleagues what the problem is. The role they play is simply to provide the necessary information rather than being involved in considering alternative solutions.
Consultative	3. You identify individuals who have useful insights and share the problem with them, getting their ideas and inputs, but doing this without bringing them together as a group. Then you make the decision, which may or may not reflect their input.
	4. You bring colleagues together and share the problem to gather their collective ideas and thoughts. However, you then still make the decision, and it may or may not reflect their influence.
Joint or group style	5. You share the problem with your colleagues as a group and you work together to come up with and then assess options. You then attempt to reach an agreement (consensus) on a solution. In this scenario, your role is much like that of a facilitator. By this, I mean that you do not try to influence the group to adopt your solution, and you need to be willing to accept and implement the decision that has the support of the group.

With this framework in mind, how do you know which style to use? This is where you then apply the diagnosis decision rules, which ask you a series of questions to then determine the appropriate decision-making style.

Leadership in practice

> ### 🛠 Toolkit item 16:
> ### The diagnosis decision rules
>
> The model suggests that you assess the situation by applying 'decision rules' to help you determine which of the five decision-making styles is appropriate. The aim is to minimise the chances of reducing decision quality and acceptance.

The question	The rules	Considerations
Is the quality of the decision important?	It's an important decision but information is missing.	If the quality of the decision is important, and you don't have enough information or expertise to solve the problem alone, then you should eliminate decision-making style 1 as a possibility.
Does your team share the company goals?	Decision quality is important, but consultation might be skewed by personal interests.	If the quality of the decision is important and colleagues are unlikely to put the interests of the organisation first, then you should eliminate 5 as an option.
Do you have all the information you need?	Decision quality is important, the decision is complex and involving others would enhance the solution.	When the quality of the decision is important but you lack the necessary information or expertise to solve the problem by yourself, and the problem is also complex and would benefit from a group interaction, then it would be wise to bring colleagues together who will likely have the necessary information. In which case, 1, 2 and 3 should be eliminated as possible methods of decision making.

Is the team commitment to the decision essential?	Decision acceptance is essential for success.	If acceptance of the decision by colleagues is critical to achieve effective implementation and you also think that it's unlikely that a decision made without consultation will be accepted, then 1 and 2 are eliminated as choices.
Is conflict over the decision likely?	Decision acceptance is critical, and colleagues are likely to disagree.	If acceptance of the decision is critical and a decision made by you is unlikely to be accepted, and disagreement among colleagues over how you achieve the organisational goal is likely, then the way you try to solve the problem needs to enable those in disagreement to resolve their differences. Under these circumstances, 1, 2 and 3 should be ruled out as they don't allow for any interaction among colleagues and would mean there is no chance for those in conflict to resolve their differences.
Is there a strong desire for staff to feel that the decision is fair and the decision is also not material enough for you to be concerned over the possible outcome?	A sense of parity and fairness is the most important aspect, and the decision is not critical.	If the quality of the decision is unimportant but acceptance is critical, and it's unlikely it would be achieved if you decide alone, then the process you go through should enable colleagues to interact and negotiate over what is the fairest way to resolve any differences. In this instance, 1, 2, 3 and 4 are eliminated from the options.

Is this a decision where you will not get support if you make it alone, and you believe staff will put the company first?	Acceptance is critical and you would benefit from colleagues feeling they have a stake in the decision.	If acceptance is critical and unlikely to result from you making the decision alone, and you feel that colleagues will be able to put the interests of the organisation first, then working on the decision in partnership with staff will likely provide greater acceptance without risking the decision quality. If so, 1, 2, 3 and 4 have to be ruled out.

You may have noticed that the first three rules are designed to protect decision quality. The remaining four rules are designed to protect decision acceptance.

This can be a little complex, but getting your head around it is helpful. Perhaps the biggest takeaway should be that you are able to, for good reasons, make decisions on your own without consulting others. This is an important leadership lesson I've learnt.

?

Are there any material decisions you've made which would have benefited from this framework? Is there anything you would have done differently when you consider these diagnosis decision rules?

Helping a group make decisions

There will often be times when the wider team or group of colleagues, or occasionally a whole organisation, need to make a decision collectively. This does not mean you need to achieve full consensus (a generally or fully accepted opinion); this would be unusual.

As a leader, you will want to play a part in facilitating a

process to enable a decision to be made, or you may wish to set up conditions to ensure a healthy debate on that decision and a mechanism to enable a decision to be reached (such as via a voting tool). In a group setting, the leadership role is to facilitate discussion in a way that both encourages others to join in and opens the group up to new alternatives if required – for example, if the conversation has become unhelpful, narrow or stuck.

These toolkit methods should help a group make a decision:

> *Toolkit item 17:*
> *Group decision making in online meetings*
>
> Online meetings enable leaders to encourage input to decisions in a range of ways. These could include:
>
> → using voting functions on your provider's chat function
> → using online tools such as Mentimeter to collect the full range of views
> → encouraging debate and input to help inform a decision, by people either expressing their views verbally in the meeting if they are happy to, or giving them in the chat.
>
> Some may find engaging in a decision-making process online frustrating and some may use it as a way to shy away from contributing. If you are chairing, you will need to juggle inviting contributions, noticing what's going on in the chat and working out the best way to reach a decision, depending on how the meeting progresses.

Leadership in practice

> 🛠 *Toolkit item 18: Creating the conditions for input to in-person meetings*
>
> With an in-person meeting where you want to gather views in order to inform a decision, you could:
>
> → encourage openness with staff by starting a meeting or workshop with an exercise that is about building trust, by starting team meetings with a personal question (see page 50)
> → include a workshop element to encourage input and mix up groups so that everyone gets an opportunity to contribute
> → make best use of your space and the fact that you are together – can you break into smaller groups and then reconvene to hear from each other?
> → start a meeting by writing up a collective group charter to try to create a safe space for working together. This might include commitments such as aiming to actively listen to others who are speaking and that discussion must be respectful, honest, supportive and open-minded.

Top tip: for any meeting format you could:

→ ask open-ended questions that your colleagues can't just answer yes or no to
→ use a 'straw person' (a rough prototype) to frame an idea or possibility for conversation to get a discussion started
→ reward and acknowledge good team working and input
→ make good use of storytelling to inspire others to generate input.

One of the biggest lessons I learnt as a new leader was to manage down my inherent desire and capacity for continuous improvement and reaching quick solutions to problems. I process quickly and often identified the problem, solution and how we would get there before my team had been given the space to fully understand and consider what the issues were. They would comply with my very specific directions, face criticism for doing things my way and I never understood why they were not as excited as I was about what we were achieving.

It took a very brave junior member of my team to help me realise that not everyone processed things as quickly as I did, and by simply providing them with a clear understanding of the end goal and then stepping back and allowing them to find their way to it would always achieve a much better outcome that the whole would embrace. I have carried that lesson with me through more than 25 years of leadership – standing in front of my team to ensure a clear destination and remaining firmly behind them as they work their way to the optimum outcome, only intervening if they looked back for support or guidance.

Using this collaborative approach to leadership has given me far more time to sweat the big stuff and helped build a series of highly effective, high-performing teams who want to consistently deliver improved results.
Dionne Spence, chief officer, General Pharmaceutical Council

Chapter reflections

I hope you are starting to get used to how this book works and are also enjoying reading the advice from other leaders. This chapter introduced quite a few Toolkit items. Did you manage to reflect on how you would use them? Have you already had a chance to put into practice some of the hints and tips for dealing with your first key meeting? Have you started engaging with strategic partners, and how confident were you after you did so?

Some essentials in this chapter, which I imagine you will return to, are the sections on effective communication and making decisions: skills that leaders continue to hone over many years. Having explored these tangible areas of leadership practice, I will now take you on to some of the more subtle leadership challenges, which require careful handling and support.

3 Dealing with some of the early leadership challenges

As a new female leader, there will be several leadership challenges you will probably experience, and it's likely that you won't be expecting them (or all of them). In my early career, I was certainly both undervalued and underestimated (by some), struggled with imposter syndrome and often compared myself to other more seemingly confident male colleagues. I found that the softer, more emotional side of these leadership challenges was hard. I hope this chapter will support you so you are ready to handle these difficulties if they arise.

Being undervalued or underestimated

This unfortunately does happen, but it doesn't mean you have to accept it. I recall being in a male-dominated team led by a strong character who used to joke about colleagues only being there to make the tea. Although this was in jest and aimed towards male and female colleagues equally, it still stung. Feeling undervalued can cause you a lot of unhappiness at work. Many people associate their personal value with how they are perceived at work, so feeling unappreciated or not respected cuts to the heart of our emotional response to our workplace.

The cause of this feeling might be extremely clear to you and is driven by signs you can't ignore. However, it might be that you're feeling this way because of a sense or gut instinct, which could be harder to address. See 'Trusting your gut', page 151, for further insights.

How to respond to being undervalued

I would like to examine a range of situations to give you some ideas about what you can do in response.

Situation: feeling that someone else takes credit for your work. There are few more frustrating moments at work than when you feel certain you have been instrumental in a piece of work or a successful outcome and then someone else takes the credit. Before you act, you should think hard about whether it truly matters and why they may have done it. However, if you can't understand it and feel it's just wrong and has caused you harm in a work setting (for example, it might be a reason you're being overlooked for a promotion), then you should find a way to raise this with the relevant person. If you have a coach, you might want to get their help with this.

Try not to be defensive: there may be a good reason that this happened, or the individual may feel that they played a bigger role in the work than you realise – and maybe they did.

I would recommend asking to speak to the person who claimed credit for your work, perhaps framing your discussion by acknowledging that this may be a bit awkward or difficult, which means that you don't raise this matter lightly. You might say that you have thought about a recent work event and are not clear why it is that they took praise or claimed credit for work you felt you led on. It's worth asking them if they can see it the same way or if they recognise the role you played and, if they did, then why they didn't acknowledge your input. It would be fair to say that you fear this lack of credit could lead to a misunderstanding about the value you bring to the company.

Early leadership challenges

If the person can't explain why they did this or won't recognise that they even did so, then this is a separate matter and I would recommend seeking further input and help, but only if you feel that this issue is detrimental to your wellbeing or standing at work. If this is something you can live with for now, you may wish to monitor the situation. If it happens again, or you think this is an ongoing issue that can't be resolved, you could assess if this is the workplace you really want to stay at. This is a last resort, however, and you should exhaust other options first, such as testing with peers or HR what their thoughts are.

Situation: not being thanked for extra effort you have made.
A bit like someone taking credit for your work, it's also frustrating when you're not thanked.

Some people are not in the habit of thanking others for their efforts. It is irritating, but it's unfortunately not unusual, and there isn't a lot you can do about the person choosing not to do it. However, what you can do is role model the behaviour you would like to see. It's essential to remember to thank others for their efforts when they have engaged with you, as hopefully that will permeate more widely, or at least will become the norm in your immediate team.

Situation: being in meetings and feeling as if your opinions are not being heard.
If it happens once, don't panic – it might be that there were other factors at play that are not about you. However, if it becomes a pattern and keeps occurring, then it's likely that you need to consider how you're coming across in meetings and what impact you're having.

I would start by thinking about whether you are communicating effectively. It might be that you feel you had a valuable point and made clear what you were thinking, but others may have heard something different or may not even have understood what you were trying to say. If you have a trusted peer, ask them afterwards whether what you felt you were communicating was what came across.

It might be that you were clear in your mind and managed to describe the idea but did not convey the intended impact. Did you clearly explain the benefits of your idea?

The key is to ensure that you're not defensive when trying to test whether you have been understood.

A further scenario is when a colleague states your exact thought at some point after you have said it. An immediate response you may want to make is: 'I just said that!' However, that may not help you and could look immature or unprofessional. Instead, you could do one of four things set out in the toolkit below (which range from the riskiest to the easiest). You will need to assess your circumstances to see which option you feel most comfortable with, and it might be that you simply don't get an option to do 1 or 2 as the time or opportunity is not afforded to you in the meeting.

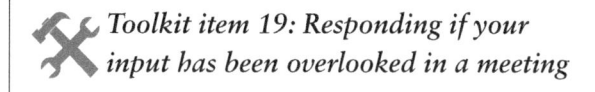

> **Toolkit item 19: Responding if your input has been overlooked in a meeting**
>
> 1. Add a further contribution later in the meeting that acknowledges your earlier input and builds on your colleague's point. However, be careful: this takes some skill and needs to be carefully handled. You could try something like: *'It was really great hearing Kevin just talk about the new work we are doing, as I feel it has given fresh insight to my earlier point on this, in that I now wonder if X or Y might work.'*
> 2. You could say something later that acknowledges your earlier point again, such as: *'I'd like to return to the comment I made earlier as I think it might be even more pertinent now because of what we have just been discussing.'*

3. After the meeting, and in private, and only if you are comfortable, you could speak to the meeting chair or your line manager to explain what happened and ask how they might recommend you be heard in the future.
4. The last option is to do nothing and accept that, unfortunately, whether intended or not, this happens to many people, and in time you'll learn how best to contribute to meetings so you feel listened to and valued. Unfortunately, some of what gives people the floor or audience in a meeting is what's known as 'position power' – they simply have a role that earns them attention and the ability to be heard.

How to respond to being underestimated

Feeling underestimated is different from being undervalued. In my experience, it has acted like fuel to my leadership journey, driving me forward because of a frustration at being underestimated and a desire to prove people wrong. However, that doesn't mean it's not harmful or frustrating. It seems to have happened to several women I know. One peer said: 'I have definitely experienced being underestimated. As I'm stubborn, it's made me want to prove myself.'

People can be underestimated for a whole range of reasons, including height, gender, hair colour, age, skin colour and upbringing, among other characteristics. I recall being a young-looking (and young) blonde (sometimes unfairly associated with being ditsy) and delighting in surprising others in meetings by waiting for the perfect moment to join in a conversation. I would think about what could be my most remarkable or insightful comment, and then input to the discussion at the moment when I would have the biggest impact. Seeing other people's faces made up for any disappointment at initially being discounted.

If you feel underestimated, you might want to think about whether any of the following give you encouragement:

→ Being underestimated is a competitive advantage – make the most of it!
→ They can't stop you if they don't see you coming.
→ I see it as an advantage to go into a negotiation being underestimated.

The most important thing to remember about underestimation is that it happens to many people, and you should never let anyone else's perception of what you can achieve contain you or limit your ambition or vision.

How you value yourself

What is it that you value most about yourself? Where do you draw your sense of value from? For some, the source of their value is derived from their appearance. For others, it may come from their capabilities and competencies, perhaps evidenced by a certificate or qualification.

When you consider how you value others, it may be that you're looking out for highly perceived levels of value, such as 'greatness' or 'genius', which seem to be what has been traditionally valued in Western work cultures. However, value can be seen in many ways. For example, attributes such as displaying kindness, warmth or openness have always seemed highly valued by colleagues, perhaps above other more obvious accolades or attributes. There has also been a societal shift in what is appreciated and valued. An article from Sussex University (the place I did my first degree!) shared that 'New research finds humility trumps arrogance in leadership success'. Tom Walters (2024) reports that the study challenges the 'conventional narrative of leadership and shows that humble leaders gain influence by lifting others up'.

In a new role, I was reflecting on what value I might bring

as a leader and did a presentation where I shared what I joked were my 'slightly boring superpowers'. These were things I saw as relatively ordinary, but have realised from experience that they may not be seen as 'just ordinary' to everyone else.

Do you have anything you can do in a work context that you feel is relatively straightforward or that you can do without too much of a challenge but have noticed that others are impressed or surprised by it? If so, they may be your own 'slightly boring work superpowers'. My list included:

→ being able to diagnose what is and isn't working in an organisation
→ designing all staff development days with creative and fun elements (see page 169).
→ being able to quickly visualise a reporting format or template and describe or create it
→ ensuring that all meetings end on time (it seems a rarity for people to do this regularly, but is greatly appreciated by colleagues)
→ keeping unread emails below ten at all times (this, I admit, is a personal choice, and perhaps a reflection of some of my need for control. However, keeping on top of emails and managing your inbox by setting up email rules will help you to be organised and feel on top of your work)
→ an ability to produce insightful, clear and concise summaries, generally verbally, of interactions, meetings or events (I realised I have an ability to draw out themes from what I have heard, identify the salient points and summarise these in a few minutes. I had thought this was fairly standard, but have come to see that it is a bit of a dark art and something that can delight others)
→ remembering what I've learnt and using it. I urge you to reflect after any noteworthy development experiences, and think about the significant learning you take away. Ideally,

note this down somewhere. I have been able to make great use of and extract a lot of value from my development activity, and found it helpful to draw on these tools, insights and learnings and apply them in my work.

What are your slightly boring superpowers? How might they bring value to your peers or team?

Remember, no two women's superpowers will be the same, which is great! As Helen shares:

We talk a lot (especially as women) about avoiding the 'curse of perfection' – but I often think the 'curse of comparison' is much worse... so my advice would be: avoid the curse of comparison, find the unique strengths that you bring to the world and harness those. When we see the world through that lens... it's amazing the opportunities it opens up.
Helen Roberts, co-founder, Talented Women

This insight about authenticity highlights an issue I talk about in my concluding text on female leadership challenges (see pages 196–8). A great author who has perfectly captured the concern I share is Monique Tallon, who in her book *Leading Gracefully* (2016) describes the incorrect assumption that to get ahead, women have come to believe they need to behave like men to be taken seriously as leaders. This is not the case, as I hope this book will help you to realise.

What to do if you doubt yourself – the imposter syndrome

I've met very few people who say they have never experienced what is known as imposter syndrome. This is when you doubt yourself, you worry you don't belong, you don't feel qualified or credible to be delivering the role that you have, or when you feel you're a fraud and expect people will identify you for the imposter that you are.

Does that sound familiar? If so, you are certainly among friends and it's something I have experienced more than once over the years.

It's important to recognise and acknowledge when you're feeling this way. This is because imposter syndrome can be draining, cause you anxiety and impact on your wellbeing, as well as your confidence at work. It's crucial to have both coping mechanisms for dealing with the feeling in the moment and regular strategies in place as part of your ongoing development to assist you with handling your leadership responsibilities.

> *Toolkit item 20:*
> *Dealing with imposter syndrome*
>
> I would advise you to:
>
> **Notice when you feel confident**
> When you feel particularly good or self-assured in your role, take note of why. How do you feel and what is making you feel confident? Make a record of your successes and acknowledge what you've achieved. If you can recognise that you're worthy in good times, it can help to look back at this if you start to doubt yourself. You could keep a small card with you that has your affirmations on it to help you acknowledge why you are an effective leader.

Examine the evidence

There will be plenty of evidence that supports why you are the right person to be in a leadership role. This could be the job offer letter you received for this post, prior appraisal or 360° feedback, acknowledgements from peers or staff members, potentially company awards or other forms of recognition. This is helpful evidence to have to hand if you feel that you're starting to doubt yourself.

Maintain your CV

It's easy to forget all that you have achieved, but keeping your CV up to date is a great way to reflect on all your accomplishments and make sure you're acknowledging the great work you're doing now. The combination of your learning and qualifications shows that you're capable and qualified to be in your role.

Accept it's natural

One tip I wanted to share is to just try living with it: internalise and acknowledge the difference between your perception of yourself and the reality others see. I remember chairing a meeting and having a strong sensation of doubt when I looked up and wondered why it was that this group of leaders were all following me and listening to my directions. Rather than panic, I smiled internally to myself and thought, 'How amazing that I have achieved this.' Noting the incredulity helped me to switch from fear to pride and move on.

Seek help

Remember you are not alone. In an organisation there are peers and colleagues who can help. Try making use of peer networks and building sufficient trust with one or more colleagues who you can turn to when needed. An effective leader is able to work with a strong team – ideally

> one with skillsets and abilities that are different from or enhance their own to help address any concerns around gaps in capability.

For me it is self-doubt. Too many of us question our abilities, but we need to recognise that our experience and knowledge, which have been earned and are now ingrained in us, will help us to overcome most situations. In addition, having the right team is crucial; none of us have all the answers and good leadership is about drawing on the expertise of others to ensure that the right decisions are made. Finally, get a mentor or a support network as sometimes, whether things are going well or not, the ability to self-reflect and talk through situations is a great learning opportunity.
Stella Marie McManus, further education college principal

Being authentic is so important. You don't need to be anything other than yourself; you don't need to try to behave in a way that you think makes you fit. And other women don't need to be perceived as a threat, so don't treat them as if they are.
Sarah Clamp, service delivery director

Always trust your intuition. If something feels off, it is. If you are in a room and you can say something and it gets dismissed and then someone else says the same thing and they are heard, then that's bias. Take it at face value. Don't let it discourage you from getting to where you want to be.
An educational leader

How to answer if someone asks you inappropriate questions

Being asked inappropriate or personal questions at work happens to most people at some point. Many inappropriate questions will be gender irrelevant, such as about your age, your ethnic background or your upbringing. However, for women, there are inappropriate questions that are gender specific. For example, if you have or are planning on having children. Men get asked this, too, but for women, it can feel like more of a loaded question as there are instances where this has (wrongly) had implications for a woman's career.

> *Toolkit item 21:*
> *Responding to inappropriate questions*
>
> When faced with a personal or inappropriate question, you might find going through these steps helpful:
>
> **Step 1**
> Consider why you are being asked this question, thinking about both the person asking the question and the context. For example, there is a lot of curiosity about a new leader, and when I started a new role, many staff wanted to know if I lived locally and whether I was planning on being in the office on a regular basis. I came across a lot of natural curiosity and didn't see any evidence that these questions were anything but innocent.
>
> **Step 2**
> If you're uncertain about the motive of the question and questioner, ask yourself: what would they gain by having this information, other than being 'in the know' about you? Can the person do anything harmful with what they might learn? Although you may have some suspicions,

I generally tend to believe that people are more likely either just being curious or wanting to be seen as having privileged information, rather than thinking that they want to do anything harmful with what they find out. However, it might be advisable to be a little cautious if you're unsure of motivations.

Step 3

It's also worth being aware of the environment you are in. Is the culture one where there is obvious openness and sharing of personal information? What do other leaders do? You should also think about where you are when answering a personal question: who might overhear your answer? Could they take the response you give out of context?

Step 4

If you're happy to answer or feel that it would be wise to respond in some way, then you have some choices. You may be happy to reply with a full answer or with a partial answer where you decide to hold some details back. Or you may feel that the best thing is to deflect the question using humour and hope the questioner realises this is your way of gently indicating that this is a question you don't feel you should answer. Or you may politely decline to give a response, perhaps citing why – for example: *'I am afraid I just don't think that is a suitable question for me to answer in a professional context; I hope you understand.'*

If you ever feel that the line of questioning is so inappropriate it has made you uncomfortable, then I would suggest seeking help from your HR team, an employee assistance programme or from an independent HR advice organisation, such as the Chartered Institute of Personnel and Development (CIPD). Remember that you have every right to personal privacy and should only reveal what you feel comfortable with, never sharing anything that you would want to keep private.

Dealing with unexpected behaviours – politics with a small p

Petty politics is a much-used phrase in workplaces. It can manifest in several ways. You might notice unkindness, inappropriate behaviour, jealous responses, gossiping, power plays and moves for control or attention, insincerity, passive-aggressive behaviour, criticism that isn't fair or clear, backstabbing or toxicity. Doesn't sound very fun, does it? Although this is something that happens in many workplaces, I've never found that it occurs across a whole workplace. (If it does, and is ingrained in a toxic workplace culture, and the tools below don't help, then run for the hills!)

I have worked at lovely places where there was minimal evidence of any of this activity, which was confined to just a few individuals, so it didn't permeate across the culture. I have also worked at places where I noticed a higher level of this conduct when I first joined, but alongside other leaders who wanted to stamp out these attitudes, it was possible to enable a culture shift to ensure that these individuals weren't given any power or credence. When you can do this, it means that those who wish to operate in this way will either adapt to the new culture, or else leave of their own accord or because a clash will result in their planned departure.

It's never easy to operate when you see evidence of this culture at play. The next Toolkit item offers some suggestions to help you.

Toolkit item 22:
Working within a toxic workplace culture

→ **Do not join in** as gossiping or backstabbing at work is not helpful and can be unkind. You will not be seen as trustworthy.

→ **Act with kindness** since role modelling a considerate approach and spreading the message of being kind to one another is a way to highlight a contrast to negative behaviour. If one of the organisational values implies or refers to supportive or caring behaviours, make use of the values to help reinforce your positive message.

→ **Challenge inappropriate behaviour**, either directly yourself when you witness it or, where necessary, make the line manager of the employee aware so that they can deal with it. Workspaces should never tolerate behaviour that intimidates, bullies or undermines others, or actions that are a cause for concern, such as a colleague taking any kind of narcotic substance at work or being involved in any fraudulent activity. There will be policies in place for dealing with inappropriate behaviour. Make use of them and follow due procedure.

→ **Be understanding** of the causes of jealous behaviour. Seek to understand why someone is behaving this way and see what the real root cause of an issue is.

→ **Do not let power plays and moves for control or attention go unnoticed**, and ensure you have the appropriate frameworks that enable greater parity for all (see page 164 for tips on leading in an inclusive way).

→ **Ignore insincerity or passive-aggressive behaviour** as giving attention to this behaviour gives it life and validity. If this becomes an ongoing problem, there are

> conduct policies you should be able to apply if required.
> → **Recognise that unfair criticism is just that: unfair.** It may be because the person is not informed or they are jealous, and the criticism may have nothing to do with you at all. Remember your value and worth. If you're not sure, get a second opinion on your work to be sure you're not being overly defensive.

It may be overwhelming if at first you find that more than one of the items on the list above apply. Don't lose hope: there will be other people who can see that this behaviour is not appropriate. Try to stay true to yourself, see if the recommended ways of responding in the toolkit above help you, and if not, seek help from your mentor or a peer.

Chapter reflections

You may not have thought about or come across all the potential challenges outlined in this chapter, or you might have experienced all the issues I have set out here during your leadership journey to date. Whatever the circumstances, I hope you now feel more fully equipped to stand up for yourself, be bold and act on your beliefs, particularly if you are undervalued or underestimated. I also wish for you that you try not to devalue yourself and that you find ways to cope if you experience imposter syndrome.

If you are currently working in a toxic workplace culture, does the tool above help you to navigate this in a better way? I also want you to feel ready to politely and firmly respond if someone asks you inappropriate questions, so make sure you return to this section whenever you need it.

Now we have covered some of the early challenges, both palpable and less tangible, I will move you on to a series of leadership tactics to enhance your confidence and capability.

4 Leadership tactics

This is a chapter which I imagine you might return to more than once, as it contains some of the most important tools and frameworks that I believe a leader needs to apply at any stage of their career. You will get to grips with tackling confrontation, how to network, appreciating the importance of effective conversations and how to handle those who want to disrupt or challenge your plans. Of all the queries I have had over the years, the topics in this chapter have been the most requested areas for support. Not only can these strategies assist you as a leader, but they can also help you to navigate your life more successfully and potentially lead to greater fulfilment and happiness.

Tackling confrontation inside and outside your organisation

Confrontation is something you cannot avoid as a leader. You will likely face it both internally with colleagues, peers, managers, maybe your board, and then you will probably deal with confrontation with external stakeholders too.

Some time ago, I was lucky enough to go on the Matthew Hussey Retreat. Matthew works with women to assist with their love lives, but he is also extremely skilled at empowering women to be their best selves, which he does in a range of ways, including through his personal development retreats. During the time I was there, a framework was shared that provided a series of considerations to use when handling confrontation in personal relationships. I found this framework very helpful and started applying an adapted version of it when tackling confrontation with work colleagues and, with permission, I'm sharing this adjusted approach here.

> **Toolkit item 23: A framework for approaching confrontation with a colleague**
>
> This approach takes you through ten steps, with questions and considerations to address.
>
> **1. Is a confrontation necessary?**
>
> → Is the result going to be productive for you or the company?
> → Is the problem significant, and does it impact on other areas of work?
> → Are you going to make the problem bigger?
> → Is it real?
> → Is there a real work problem or is this about your professional relationship instead?
> → Does it need to be you who addresses this or do you need to alert someone else to this issue? People often create confrontation by putting themselves in situations that aren't their concern.
>
> **2. Focus on the outcome – what's the result I want from this?**
>
> → What outcome would you like to achieve and how will it benefit the team or organisation?
> → Think two moves ahead – what does this lead to?

→ What are the possible outcomes from the discussion? You must be comfortable with all possible eventualities that might result for you and for the company. Have a strategy for each of the possible outcomes if you can.

3. Choose the right time to have the discussion you need to have

→ Early is better: in the day, in the process, in the relationship, in the issue.

4. Stay neutral

→ When you confront, you need clarity; therefore, you must not let emotions confuse the situation. As a leader, you should also be able to manage your feelings in a professional setting.

→ The colleague you are talking to needs to understand why you are having this discussion and that there is an issue to address. If you give an emotional response, that will cloud both of your abilities to see the issue clearly.

→ Don't rush to be judgemental.

5. Choose the right setting

→ Where should your discussion take place? Is there a regularly occurring diary event when you'll have a chance for a private conversation? There will be in-person private spaces you can use, or if you're on a video call, make sure you can't be overheard.

→ If you're going to challenge or criticise someone, do so in private – this helps build the trust between you and hopefully means that the person is less likely to be defensive. The more trust you have built up with someone, the easier it is to have a confrontation.

→ On the flip side, make sure you praise in public: value

escalates in direct proportion to the number of people who hear it.

6. Employ the sandwich technique (if appropriate)

→ Start with praise, but make sure it's genuine. Then raise the issue, be clear it's about solving a problem, and end with praise again if you can.
→ When the professional situation is difficult, showing kindness and humanity is important.

7. Use 'we' and not 'you'

→ 'You' causes defensiveness. Confrontation can feel like finger pointing, and using 'you' can lead to your colleague becoming argumentative.
→ Use language like 'we have a problem', 'how are we going to solve the problem?'.
→ It's important to be on the same team.

8. Communicate why this is important

→ Your colleague may not recognise the problem as you see it, so don't assume that they understand there's an issue.
→ Be as articulate and concise as you can about the reason this matters.

9. Create the expectation

→ Plan the outcome together. This will increase the likelihood of success. What will be different? What are you both hoping will change?
→ Ask how you can help: how can I make this work?
→ See if any support is needed and provide it where you can.

10. Confirm the discussion

→ It's helpful to have an agreed record of what you have

Leadership tactics

> discussed, but make sure you reinforce the positive, such as, *'It's great we had this conversation. Thanks for your reaction – we have a plan together.'*

It's worth recognising that some people are confrontational as a way of working. I've had more than one colleague (mainly men) who has told me they find conflict beneficial for creativity or problem solving. It's their preferred method for testing assumptions to see if ideas may be faulty, or to work through problems by debating them with a colleague to weigh up options. What's important is to not take this personally. I also find it's a good idea to have a conversation about how you work best together (see suggestions on page 27), to understand how confrontational a relationship will be and prepare yourself for how you will respond.

Confrontation with external stakeholders

My advice here is to always be professional and maintain your standards. I've found that issues with external stakeholders are harder to address or resolve after the event than those with internal colleagues, so handling confrontation well in the moment is essential.

> *Toolkit item 24: Handling confrontation with external stakeholders*
>
> → **Understand the problem.** What has led to this conflict? What is the root cause of the issue? Do you have all the information you need? If not, where can you get more information? In the heat of the moment, you may need to calmly ask the other party if they could set out for you the exact nature of the issue, making it clear that you want to understand them fully. Ask open-ended questions, ensure you listen carefully

and seek clarity where you need to. Be kind and empathetic, as this will help in getting to the bottom of the problem.

→ **Be professional at all times.** Keep calm, do not use emotive language, do not raise your voice, be patient and make sure you communicate your points as clearly and concisely as possible. I was once on a stakeholder call with other leaders in the sector I worked in. They were all acting in a more assertive and challenging way than I was, and I think the contrast became a little embarrassing for them. They apologised, saying, 'We're not having "a go" at you.' My professional approach enabled me to know that I had not dropped my leadership standards. It took the heat out of the discussion and meant we could have a more productive exchange.

→ **Try not to disagree.** In his excellent book *The Diary of a CEO* (2023), the entrepreneur and *Dragon's Den* investor Steven Bartlett suggests this as an effective response tactic, as telling someone they are wrong is inflammatory. Instead, try to find ways to appease, for example by recognising that although they have a point, you don't see it that way; instead, you're wondering if (insert your point) is the case instead. Finding common ground is essential. Consider what you can agree on; it will help if you start with agreement. With external stakeholders, you might be aiming for the same end outcome, but you may not agree on the methodology to achieve those aims. Seeing if you can agree on the bigger picture can make the discussion easier.

→ **Are you the right person to address this?** Sometimes as a leader you may be caught in a moment of conversation with a stakeholder when a matter comes up and you're not best placed to address it. You may not have all the knowledge you need, or the decision-making authority to satisfactorily agree a resolution. Be aware of this and don't over-commit or provide only part of the solution. If this is the case, it's better to get further input. Be wary as well: sometimes a stakeholder may know that you're not quite the right person to address an issue but might be hoping to agree something with you that another member of your organisation would not agree to.

→ **Be collaborative**. The advice above on internal conflict was to use 'we' not 'you', and I would suggest following this step with external stakeholders too. I would also advise you to follow the recommendation about co-creating the next steps if you are able to.

→ **Check on the satisfactory conclusion of the issue**. Make sure you follow up after the event, to see if the solution you have applied is working and whether the issue is satisfactorily resolved. If it isn't, it may require further discussion or action. If you don't check, you may think that a matter is resolved, while instead the issue escalates and becomes a bigger problem.

Building networks

Building effective networks both inside and outside your organisation will be extremely useful to you. In my experience, this is one of the most common things that even established leaders still struggle with.

Why do you need a network?

Internally, having colleagues you can rely on, share ideas with and get constructive feedback from is invaluable. It makes your role easier. I also find that knowing the best person or team to undertake a specific task, or where to get ideas on a specialist subject, will make you more effective at your role.

Having networks and positive relationships at work is important for your wellbeing and the enjoyment of your job. If you have good connections and know where expertise in the business lies, you're likely to be more effective when it comes to collaborating with others and more successful and productive in the output of that work. This enables you to alleviate some of the stresses of your role, which should lead to greater levels of job satisfaction.

Externally, establishing good connections with those you admire, wish to learn from, want to work with or who have influence in your sector is highly valuable. You can build these networks in a variety of ways, such as attending learning and development events, conferences, awards ceremonies, formal meetings and other occasions that gather leaders from across sectors together. I have also used social media, especially LinkedIn, to extend my professional network.

Networking at one of these occasions is not always easy and is something that you may find challenging or uncomfortable. Here are some ways in which you might approach a networking event.

Tips for attending a networking event

Think about how you will approach the event before you go. Who are the attendees? Is there anyone you want to make sure you talk to? What can you learn about them in advance, so you have some talking points when you meet? What are your personal goals for the event – are you looking to explore an opportunity, widen your contacts, potentially talk to someone about a role? Think about the setting: what will be the most appropriate business dress to wear? How will you get there so you're not late or flustered when you arrive?

During the event, be bold and confident. Perhaps you need to apply your alter ego – like Beyoncé Pad Thai (see page 74). Remember that others are in the same boat as you and may also find this difficult. Try to circulate rather than stand on the sidelines.

Greeting people. This is about demonstrating confidence (even if inside you're not feeling it): looking someone in the eye, putting out your hand for a handshake and being open and friendly and introducing yourself. If you can, have something further you can add that is relevant to them. For example, '*I was interested to read that your organisation is using AI to predict weather patterns to help address climate change. How is that going?*' Or I find that it's OK to flatter people as part of an introduction, such as, '*I was impressed by your article on climate change – what got you into this work?*' All you need is a starting point and then hopefully the conversation can flow.

Joining in a conversation. People don't mind if you walk up to a gathering and stand there quietly, smiling and just listening. In nearly every case, our instinct is to create space and widen the group to allow others to join. Wait for the right time to contribute and then, when you see an opening, introduce yourself and pick up on something that has been discussed. It would be highly unusual for you to be rejected in this scenario. However, if you come across unkind people who don't widen their circle or enable you to join in, don't be disheartened – try somewhere else.

Be organised. If you have a mobile phone with you and are on LinkedIn, you can easily share your contact details by opening the app, selecting the search function and clicking on the small QR code symbol. This brings up your LinkedIn QR code for anyone to save using the camera on their phone. It's the modern-day business card. However, there's nothing wrong with using a traditional business card if that works for you. Keep a record of key points or individuals you have talked to and follow up with the contacts you meet by connecting on LinkedIn or via email. If you feel it would be beneficial, you may wish to arrange a follow-up call or meeting.

Network, network, network! Individuals you meet through business networks may have been there before or could be going through a similar experience so can add valuable advice and insights around challenging problems. Building a network to share your experiences can provide you with encouragement, support and guidance along your leadership journey.
Amanda Foreshaw, HR lead, strategic business partner and leadership coach

Life and leadership isn't a straight line – downs will follow ups but ups will also follow downs... harness the power of support networks to help you grow through both...
Helen Roberts, co-founder, Talented Women

The art of conversation

I feel it's vital that leaders know how to have good conversations and understand what conversations can achieve and why they're essential for effective leadership. If you've only ever seen conversations as a form of communication, or haven't really thought about them, then I would urge you to see them as a vehicle for so much more.

Conversations allow you to be curious, to explore and to investigate. They are an enabler to help **increase your understanding** about a person, an issue or a subject. Although conversations are an exchange or an interaction, some can be rather one sided; the person who dominates the conversation leads the narrative and may not allow the other person to interject to fully understand what they are saying. I advise you to approach a discussion with a curious mindset, actively listen to what the other person is saying, use the discussion to test what you're hearing and respond with insightful questions to increase your comprehension.

Having a conversation allows you to **find solutions to problems**. Too often, we can be pressed for time and may sometimes feel we're the only ones with the insight we have on an issue, narrowing our solution design. Or it may be that we're reluctant to demonstrate vulnerability by sharing a half-formed idea or showing that we don't have all the answers. To remedy this, take the time to find someone appropriate to have a conversation with, as this enables you to find new wisdom, helps you by getting you to talk through your thinking and requires you to be open to questions and to provide explanations, which should lead to you gaining clarity. A further benefit is that through testing your understanding with colleagues, it will help them feel trusted, valued and respected.

Conversations with a **high degree of listening** involved (on your part) ensure that you don't end up with a bias or make assumptions that don't take account of the bigger picture. Listening is an important part of a conversation: making sure you hear (and understand the detail of) what's being said, not just the words that are spoken, and looking out for any indicators or undertones that might paint a different picture. This is particularly relevant when you're starting a new role, as it's likely you will have preconceived ideas and assumptions, and these may not be correct. Being mindful to engage in conversations with an intention to listen more than you contribute will help you gather as much intelligence as possible and get a good feel for the organisational climate and culture.

Conversation is also important when it comes to tackling confrontation (see page 103) or **negotiating successful outcomes** to issues. Talking through an issue to keep refining and reflecting on a problem and working towards a solution is essential for negotiating successful and peaceful outcomes.

There are lots of good reasons to value conversation, but it's not always easy, particularly when you're **facilitating a discussion**. The tool below will help you to lead a conversation well.

> ⚒ *Toolkit item 25:*
> *Making the most of a conversation*
>
> These recommendations can help you to have an effective conversation, enabling you to increase your understanding, find solutions to issues, gain all the relevant details and create a successful outcome.
>
> → Try to find the right time and place for a discussion, and make sure that it's in a setting where you will be able to concentrate.
> → Be patient, practise being able to listen with genuine interest and be present in the conversation so you're taking note of what is said and what is unsaid.
> → As another person is talking, take a mental note of key points to return to. When you can, pick up on points from the discussion: it will demonstrate that you have been actively listening.
> → A good conversation evolves. Try to come up with ways to expand and move the conversation through connected topics and thoughtful questions.
> → As a leader, your role is to ensure that the conversation remains inclusive and respectful. If a few individuals are taking over, aim to widen the discussion to increase the participation of others, facilitate where needed and negotiate the pitfalls that may arise when discussing challenging subjects.
> → When necessary, you may need to use humour to create a sense of enjoyment and lighten the mood. Or

Leadership tactics

> you may find that the best tactic is to suggest a break and breather to enable people to reset and then carry on the discussion.
> → If you need to ensure that the conversation stays exploratory and open minded, you could use the 'Steering a new conversational direction' tool (page 145).

Handling dissenters, dementors and disrupters

Leaders will face those who do not agree with their direction of travel or that of the organisation. Such people may actively provide dissent, defined by the Cambridge Dictionary as 'giving a strong difference of opinion on a particular subject, especially about an official suggestion or plan or a popular belief'. They may act as a dementor, described by J K Rowling in *The Prisoner of Azkaban* (1997) as those who drain all the happiness, hope and peace out of a situation, so that if you get too near one, all your positivity will be sucked out of you! It may sound dramatic, but I've certainly met some significant positivity drainers when trying to implement change. A different kind of challenger is a disrupter: a person who interrupts an event, activity or process by causing a disturbance or problem.

None of these are easy to deal with. I've often experienced this kind of reaction from some staff when I have been leading change, which is unsurprising given that this is when you're likely to experience the strongest reactions from those not aligned with your direction. As one colleague put it to me, 'Change is everyone's friend until it impacts them personally; then it's a bad idea.'

It's important not to become too disheartened; change elicits a strong response from staff. This next tool offers considerations and tips you could apply.

Toolkit item 26:
Working with dissenters, dementors or disrupters

→ **Listen closely to their objections** – there may be merit in what these individuals are feeling; they could see an issue in a way that you haven't considered. Don't make the mistake of just dismissing what's being said. Instead, find a time to listen to these individuals and take their points into account. It's up to you to then critically assess whether there's value in their objections. Remember, by giving them airtime, it can take some of the wind out of their sails.

→ **Seek clarity on their objections** – ask questions, listen carefully, follow up and be unemotional. Try to fully investigate what the root cause of their issue is.

→ **Aim for connection** – building common ground will help with achieving alignment. Be careful not to just argue your point of view without doing the steps above. You may need to challenge something that's clearly incorrect, or you might need to do some myth-busting if some false assumptions are prevailing. If so, do this in a calm and clear way, as it might also alleviate some of the tension.

→ **Harness the strength of their feeling** – people who are prepared to challenge in this way feel strongly about the work they're doing. This can be a good thing. Acknowledge their enthusiasm and passion, then consider how you can you turn that negativity into positivity and those individuals from detractors into champions of the work. A way to do this it so to say, 'It's great that you feel so strongly about this – will you help me achieve this goal?'

→ **Bring challengers close to the heart of the work** – I've found that appointing some of the challengers as members of the change group is a successful way

to mitigate against what could potentially become a spread of negativity. This must be carefully managed. Splitting up those who dissent and putting them in different groups alongside positive change champions can be useful. Empowering them through giving them a role in the work and helping them to hopefully see the benefits will assist you in addressing this issue.
→ **Be mindful of your resilience and wellbeing** – working with objectors can be challenging and tiring. Think about how you manage your wellbeing (see page 153 for tips on wellbeing).
→ **Do not get sidetracked** – keep the faith in what you're doing, especially if you have explored all possible objections and identified that you can address the legitimate concerns through your work. Try to maintain your positivity and draw on those who are the ambassadors of this work to help support you. If you want to check whether you have assessed the situation correctly, get a second opinion to be sure you're not being overly defensive.

Leading with influence

Leaders have a key influencing role, in part because of their position in the organisation, and in many cases because they have essential influencing skills. Leaders will influence in several ways:

→ Making things happen. Sometimes only a leader can create the momentum or initiate the action to make things happen. Ideally, this should not consistently be the case, and if people are CC-ing you regularly into emails to ensure that an action happens, then you may need to look at why there is a culture where colleagues don't respond to one another.

→ **Setting conditions for a successful project.** As a leader, you'll have an overview of a piece of work that may have multiple stages and contributors. You can therefore influence how successfully the work comes together. For example, if you know there's a key person who needs plenty of thinking time, you can speak to them in advance so they can start to do their preparation. You may be relying on an external partner for input, in which case taking the lead to put in place protocols and clear timelines with penalties for any delays should help. You can also set the tone for harmonious and effective working by, for example, drawing up a team charter for the work.

→ **Shaping organisational culture.** Leaders play a key role in reinforcing organisational culture and ways of working within a company. Embodying the organisational values and actively referring to them through the delivery of your work helps to reinforce the attributes that the organisation wishes to demonstrate in its operations. Exploring with your team how you actively demonstrate the values and behaviours in your work will help to align staff with the company culture.

→ **Communicating organisation strategy and messages.** Leaders have a responsibility to deliver company communications in the way they're intended and can ensure that messaging is managed with the appropriate tone. Leaders should publicly be supportive of company directives. Staff will notice leaders who don't seem to agree with a company direction. How you deliver important messages, with sincerity and backing, will have an influence on how they are received and whether they are acted on.

→ **Impacting on staff wellbeing.** Having awareness of your staff and their welfare, showing consideration for their personal circumstances and understanding how your behaviour might have an impact on their wellbeing will make a big difference to whether staff trust you, follow you, support you and feel comfortable being open and transparent with you.

→ **Influencing levels of clarity and understanding.** Staff need to understand the core purpose of their roles, their contribution to the team and the boundaries within which they should operate. It's the duty of a leader to provide clarity and ensure that staff can perform to the best of their abilities. This can be done in several ways, including providing guidance and frameworks for others to follow, being consistent with the application of changes or directives, having clarity on team roles (perhaps using the RACI model; see page 59) and ensuring that role profiles or job descriptions and associated objectives are relevant and current, so that staff are being assessed against the appropriate core requirements.

→ **Influencing others to operate within a culture of accountability.** While a leader will have overarching accountability for the work of their team, staff members in that team might be responsible for specific deliverables and will require sufficient autonomy to deliver the outcomes expected. Helping staff to feel empowered and emphasising that you're confident in their ability to lead the work will support an accountability culture. Sometimes leaders need to delegate because undertaking the task is an important part of their colleagues' learning and development. Unless there's a reason not to, leaders need to trust their colleagues to deliver and avoid micromanagement, which can cause dissatisfaction and discouragement.

→ **Fostering a learning culture at work.** Look for opportunities to develop individuals and the team. Encourage staff to have a continuous improvement mindset and invest in their own formal and informal learning. Leading by example, ensuring you keep your own knowledge current on your subject matter and on how to be a great leader, will help with your credibility as a leader who supports learning and development. For example, I recently organised for staff in my team to receive a book that enhanced our collective understanding of change, and I also provided an academic article to underpin this learning with theory.

→ **Encouraging others to have feedback loops where they get to recognise success.** Have you ever felt as if you needed to have a sense of achievement and then you did something well and got that feeling of satisfaction? Do your team get a chance for that same sense of satisfaction? It might be that staff are working on a longer project, or experiencing a challenging period of work, and there may be few 'wins'. What can you do about this? You can influence as a leader by recognising smaller achievements, or milestones or less obvious gains, to help create a sense of progress. You can make sure you're helping your staff to see how their work has contributed to organisational successes or more publicly recognise their contribution to your work.

→ **Acting as a role model to others.** Remember, leaders are more visible to staff than those who don't have that responsibility. Others will be guided by how you behave. Staff might also use you as a role model for how they want to operate in the future. As a female leader, is it vital to recognise the importance of being a role model and to not underestimate how valued that is by your female colleagues. I have been fortunate to be told by more than one younger woman at work that they are pleased to work in an organisation with a female leader as it makes it possible for them to recognise that they might also be a leader in the future. I should also add here that men can make excellent role models for women too!

Prioritisation and delegation

Many new leaders (and some well-established ones) find it hard to delegate and prioritise their work. A useful time management model that picks up on both these aspects is the '4 Ds' concept. This originated from the Eisenhower Matrix, developed by President Dwight Eisenhower to help him prioritise and deal with the high-stakes issues he faced as a US Army general and was popularised by Stephen Covey in *The 7 Habits of Highly Effective People* (1989). This is a popular strategy for helping leaders (or any staff) to consider their work and split it into one of four Ds.

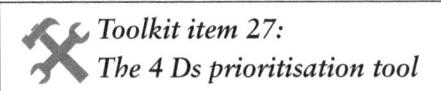

> *Toolkit item 27:*
> *The 4 Ds prioritisation tool*
>
> → Do
> → Defer (Delay)
> → Delegate
> → Delete (Drop)
>
> The aim is to critically assess your work, either looking ahead at a task list or using it more spontaneously in the moment to quickly decide how to act. Either is beneficial. You can decide whether or not you think you need to **do** the work now, or if you don't need to do it immediately, you can **defer** the work, or you can consider whether it might be good if you were to **delegate** the activity (more on that below), or if you should **delete** or drop it from your list as it's no longer needed.

Having a grid with the four quadrants and working through your 'to do' list with this in mind is a useful way to make sure you are directing your efforts where they are most needed and only on essential activities.

A quick tip on deferring work – remember it is essential to schedule immediately when you are deferring or delaying till, otherwise you could end up with an increasingly large list of deferred items which do not get addressed!

Delegation

Why should you delegate? There are many good reasons:

→ You have too much to do, but the work is time critical and needs to happen now.
→ You could do this work, but it would be a useful learning opportunity for another person to do it.
→ You share the learning and the successful outcome if you delegate all or some of the work. This builds trust between you and the relevant team members.
→ Someone might simply do the work better than you, as they could bring a deeper understanding or insight to the work or have a skillset that means they will produce a better output.

Many leaders fall into the habit of thinking that they are the only person who can undertake a task, so there's no choice but for them to do it. Have you heard someone say *'I would delegate, but it will take too long to explain and I may as well do it myself'*? You may still be the best person to do the work, but unless someone is given a chance, they will never learn how to be as effective as you at this task, and you will always be in the same position. Acting this way also makes you a blocker to work being completed because it only rests with you. Take the person you're delegating to through what's needed and how you have done this in the past. It may be a little time consuming at first, but it's worth it to save time in the future.

?

Could you be more effective in your delegation? Would you try using the 4 Ds model?

Chapter reflections

Do you now feel more equipped to handle a range of situations with the leadership skill, diplomacy, tact and careful handling that's needed? Earlier chapters looked at your interface with others, whereas this one has zeroed in on you as a leader and some of the solo leadership challenges you have to deal with, from handling confrontation or being bold at networking events to leading with influence and ensuring you prioritise effectively. The next chapter shifts to management, but as this is a leadership book, I will concentrate on the strategic elements of the management relationships you have to lead.

5 Managing others

I decided that it would be helpful to include a chapter that explores a range of management responsibilities from a leadership perspective. In my career, I have managed mixed teams, dealt with underperformance, had the unfortunate role of having to move staff out of the business and have learnt how to manage effective meetings. I'm going to share my approaches and insights on all these different management experiences – starting with your manager, which is one of the most important management relationships you will have. That sounds odd, doesn't it? They manage you, surely?! They do, but as you'll see, I believe that a good leader also manages their manager.

Managing your manager

By this point in your career, you may well have realised that the management relationship with your line manager is two way. As well as your line manager managing you, you in turn will need to manage your relationship with them.

Toolkit item 28:
Managing your manager considerations

These are a number of approaches that I've found to be effective:

→ **Managing them to enable you to deliver your work.** This could include needing their sign-off for something. One way to manage this is to pre-warn them: *'I have a contract that will need your authorisation on Wednesday. When would you need to receive it to enable that to happen please?'* Another situation would be when you need them to approve something so you can move forward with a piece of work. Agreeing with your manager how you both like to work and knowing how your manager likes to be engaged with in these circumstances is invaluable.

→ **Preparing a discussion topic list for your meetings.** I've found it useful to share a list of agenda items with my manager in advance of our interactions so that we both know I am hoping we can cover in the time we have. I make sure to check early in our relationship if they're happy to work in this way. Some managers might not like this approach, so although you may not send the list, it doesn't mean that you couldn't still organise yourself this way to know what you would like to cover when you meet.

→ **Working through issues you're jointly facing.** There will undoubtedly be times when you're undertaking a piece of work that your manager also has a role in. They may be the accountable person who has ownership of the task, and you might be the responsible deliverer of the activity. Whatever the circumstances, it's worth agreeing how you'll work together specifically on that activity. Would you need to have separate meetings to discuss the work further to your usual one-to-ones? Would you want to review progress more frequently? Taking the initiative to agree a way of working can be useful, particularly if an issue arises and you need to convene specifically to discuss it.

→ **Escalating matters of concern to your manager.** This could be on staffing issues, strategic concerns, problems with a major piece of work, press or media challenges, among other matters. As part of establishing your working relationship, it's wise to agree with your manager what types of issues they would wish to hear about, and how best to contact them if they do.

→ **Asking for their help.** As a leader, you will want to take responsibility and accountability for your work. However, there are times when you might need help and a steer to ensure you're fulfilling the expectations your manager has of you. It's better to do this early in any task or delivery of an objective to ensure you're not going down a path that will be unhelpful. Even if you feel you're fully equipped and have all the insights you need to deliver on an activity, it's worth recognising the knowledge and insights your manager will have, given their prior experience. Acknowledging this through seeking their input will help build a relationship of trust. Showing some vulnerability is healthy, too, as it can help your manager realise that you feel comfortable asking for their help when needed.

→ **Avoid making assumptions.** A coach asked me a great question recently: 'What are you assuming about your manager?' I realised I was making assumptions about what they wanted to know from me, how much detail they needed and what decisions I thought they wanted input on. Asking and being clear about this will help you to manage your manager's needs. Questions such as: '*I am going to complete the report*

> we discussed by next Thursday – do you want to see it before it gets circulated more widely or are you happy for it to go straight out?' Or, 'I asked for your input to these decisions recently – do you feel they were decisions that you would wish to have contributed to?'

It is important to remember that these meetings with your manager are not just about moving things forward; they are also a representation of how you are performing and how you are undertaking your role. The items you discuss should be proportionate to how you are spending your time at work. That may mean around 80 per cent of your meeting is talking about things you have accomplished and are addressing as a means of updating on progress or providing key information your manager needs to be aware of. Then only about 20 per cent are things you need help from your manager on. There are two good reasons for this. First, your manager will need to report upwards on the activities in your area. Second, your manager may think otherwise that you are only bringing them problems rather than having an understanding of all you have accomplished.

I'm now going to cover the dynamics of managing both women and men. This topic is well explored in books such as Judy Wajcman's *Managing Like a Man: Women and Men in Corporate Management* (2013), which is based on a major study of five multinational corporations with model equality policies and considers the workplace and management gender differences.

Managing other women

I have separated out managing women from managing men as I think women managing women is a relatively new paradigm, given the more recent rise in female leaders, and I've been told by others that this can be a complicated relationship they wish they'd had more insight on. I should note that not all women are the same, and there isn't one perfect answer on how to work together as two female colleagues. However, in speaking to other female leaders, I am aware that there are some differences that people have experienced, with distinct advantages and disadvantages to managing male colleagues.

Advantages to managing women

→ Women can often understand each other's need for time flexibility in a more unique way, given their lived experience. This applies directly to women who have children or other caring responsibilities; however, women may also have gained understanding from friends and relatives or from reading or knowing about challenges that these women are facing.
→ Women seem to be able to effectively multitask more intuitively and can achieve a lot together.
→ Women tend to draw on a range of insights and intuition to be effective in work, including emotional, intellectual and spiritual strength, and knowing this makes managing other women easier.

Disadvantages to managing women

→ Although women can understand the circumstances other women face, it can sometimes mean that they are tougher on other women because they themselves have had to navigate menstruation, childcare, menopause, etc and may have coped in a different way, which could include handling these aspects with greater ease, which could in turn lead to them sometimes being less supportive than men.
→ Some women may use the concept of 'sisterhood' to ask you to bend the rules beyond what you feel is appropriate.

→ I've seen some women be more visible in their emotional response to work decisions and issues. This can be challenging when trying to address issues in a considered way.
→ Women can sometimes forge professional relationships and mistake them for more personal friendships.
→ Women still face a range of challenging personal issues that they need to address in addition to managing their work responsibilities, and those may not always be obvious, so it can be hard to understand what tough issues your staff member may be facing, as outlined by Susan below.

Despite the progress made in terms of societal attitudes and legislation and in workplaces towards equality and inclusion, many of these subjects still feel taboo. Dealing with issues such as pregnancy, infertility treatment, balancing caring responsibilities, menopause symptoms and lack of self-confidence in the workplace continues to be extremely challenging for many women.

It can be daunting for team members to raise issues often experienced by women in the workplace with their manager, even if they are female. Providing an opening for this discussion, understanding they are not alone in experiencing these issues and (sharing that) as a manager you can provide support can significantly reduce anxiety. Stories are very powerful, be they your own experience or those of other women, and can be a springboard for this discussion. Be sensitive in your approach – be aware that not everyone experiences these issues or wants to discuss these openly with a manager.

Susan Hamilton, hospice CEO and non-executive director in housing and health

Managing men

Managing men can be great for women but can also be a challenge. This partly depends on your approach and on the attitude of the male colleagues towards you.

In my career, I've had great experiences managing men and have worked with male colleagues who have no issues whatsoever being managed by a female boss. I'm aware that this is not always the case, although that kind of old-fashioned thinking is thankfully dying out.

The advantages and disadvantages of managing men are in some ways the flip side of managing women:

Advantages to managing men

- → Things feel generally more straightforward; there seems to be more formality to the professional relationship.
- → Men seem less drawn, in general, to display emotions in work; however, there are disadvantages to this as I outline below.
- → Men seem better at having work friends without the extra complications or heightened expectations of what that connection means. I tend to think men are better at realising that friendship is earned over time and that they shouldn't put high expectations on new connections.

Disadvantages to managing men

- → Men can be less understanding or informed about some of the responsibilities that women deal with daily, or with the challenging personal issues women face, such as dealing with menopause. This is not all men, however. I've worked with highly empathic male bosses, and it's also not always women who have most of the home life responsibilities.

→ I have seen less visible emotional responses from male colleagues to work issues, although that's not to say that I haven't seen strong emotions from men in work settings. It could be that men feel just as passionately about an issue as women do, but may mask some emotions from you, which can make it harder as a manager to determine when there are issues that really matter.

→ Several men I've worked with have struggled to multitask in the way I have seen women doing. There are both pros and cons to this. In some ways, it means male colleagues can apply a more singular focus to a piece of work. However, if there are multiple competing and pressing priorities, there can be challenges for male colleagues to be as proficient at this, with some women not fully understanding why men aren't able to juggle work in the same way.

There are clearly advantages and disadvantages to managing men and women and neither is better than the other. I've had wonderful and rewarding work relationships with both genders.

Managing and relationships at work

What I haven't covered in discussing either managing women or men are potentially inappropriate or more personal relationships between work colleagues. These are certainly not uncommon, and many people meet their partners at work. There should ideally be company guidance about relationships at work, and if there isn't, you may need to understand the implications if you begin a relationship with a colleague. Be aware as well that, as a leader, and particularly as a female leader, if you're in a work relationship, you may face heightened scrutiny and will need to do all you can to provide assurance that there will be no issue in adhering to company policies. I know this as I met my partner at work and made sure that all relevant parties were informed immediately and that we were not breaching any company rules.

Managing a strong team

Recruiting and building the best team

You could inherit a team that is at full headcount, you may have gaps in your team to fill, or you might find you're building a team from scratch. If you're not currently recruiting a team, you could return to this section in the future when you are. If you have a remit to undertake some recruitment, make use of internal guidance and follow all HR processes.

As this is a book for leaders, I want to explore how you take practical steps to ensure the most positive appointment of an individual who is going to succeed as a member of your team.

My advice is:

→ **Think carefully before you put out a job advert.** Is the role the right one? If this is a role someone has left, is it still needed? Do you need to reconsider how you frame the role or shape the team? Are you setting someone up for failure if the role is flawed?

→ **Look underneath the surface of the CV and cover letter.** When producing your shortlist, remember that some people might tick all the boxes, have glittering accolades or have worked at some fancy brand names, but you need to take time to explore the story of their career. How have they invested in themselves? What experience shows you that they have the capability to be excellent in this role? What do you need from the role now, and what will you need in 18 months or three years, and does the individual demonstrate an ability to evolve and grow as the company does?

→ **In the interview, pay close attention to what they say, how they behave and how you respond to them.** Be careful not to operate with unconscious bias, where you might be tempted to pick people you will get along with or who have a similar background to you. Don't go for obvious candidates; you can teach the subject matter, but not necessarily the attitude, skills or mindset.

Remember a team is a collective, and you want it to function well, with a good balance of skills, backgrounds, insights, perspectives and capabilities as well as diversity of thought.

Representing and championing your team

As a leader you will be representing your team within the organisation. This means that you will need to do a few things:

→ **Recognise the accountability you have for the work of your team** and the fact that you represent the team with other colleagues in the organisation. Be the contact point for queries or issues to be raised, or tasks assigned and work requested.
→ **Address any issues that arise from the work of your team,** lead on solution design and alert any other teams or individuals that might be impacted by the issues you are dealing with.
→ **Never act defensively when receiving feedback about your team** or a member of your team. It's right to clarify, ask questions and understand the details of any criticism or challenge, and if you can, correct the issue immediately with a response or explanation. However, you may need to commit to come back to the individual(s) with a response.
→ **Alert colleagues to any pressures your team is under.** Think ahead and consider the pipeline of work. If there are pressing deadlines that might mean your team can't

provide the same service and input to the rest of the organisation as usual, or if challenges such as sickness and absence are going to affect the team's work or that of others, then you will need to let colleagues know.
→ **Ensure that the team has clarity** on the part it plays in contributing to the organisation's mission and objectives.
→ **Champion your staff** by raising awareness of their successes and contribution to positive outcomes. Ensure you never take credit for their work – it can be a major demotivator.
→ **Manage the impact of change on your team.** Consider the implications of any organisational change, restructures or systems changes on your team and plan ahead where you can.
→ **Ensure that your team collaborates with others.** Ask questions like, how does our work affect others? Who else do we need to consult with to achieve our work? Who else do we need to inform about the intended outputs of our work?

?

How effectively do you feel you represent and champion your team? Could you be responding differently when you reflect on the list above?

In my early working career, I was led by a director who looked ahead at least a year in advance at government policy and possible contracts and tenders that might be coming up, and when we had a significant opportunity on the horizon, he asked us to conduct a workshop on what it might mean for our team. This ensured we were always well prepared and had a considered response at the point when we needed to act.

Managing underperformance in your team

It's highly likely that during your leadership experience you will have a member – or more than one – of a team you are responsible for who is not performing to the standards and levels that you expect or that the organisation is looking for.

This is not easy. However, it's essential to address performance issues, as if they're not handled, it can have negative consequences for you and for your team, such as:

→ You may be seen as a leader who is unable to address and resolve performance issues.
→ Your team may miss critical deadlines or be unable to fulfil expectations.
→ You may be relying on input from a team member to hit one or more of your deadlines, which might cause you a delay.
→ Other staff may have to overwork to compensate for poor performance, which can lead to burnout, demotivation and, worst case, losing a good employee – which exacerbates the issue.
→ A negative impact on team morale and wellbeing.

This is certainly not an exhaustive list of possible issues; there are other ramifications I've not included here. With that in mind, addressing an issue with performance is essential and doing so as soon as the issue arises is vital.

Your company should have policies and procedures in place for how you work through a process of addressing performance issues. It will be important to make use of these and seek guidance if you're not sure how to apply them. However, before you move to a formal procedural stage, I want to help you with tackling this issue more informally first.

Addressing underperformance as a line manager (informal approach)

If you can address underperformance before it gets to a formal process, you may be able to avoid that step. My advice is to have a meeting with the relevant individual, in an appropriate setting, and make sure you prepare well in advance. Think about the main issues you want to raise and whether you have any supporting information you would want to share with them. Although this is an informal process, it is still worth involving HR at this stage to keep them updated on the actions you are taking and get any advice or input.

In the meeting, I like to make it clear that we are getting together because I would like to discuss how they are performing. If there's a widespread issue with their performance, you might keep your opening question at a general level, such as *'Can you tell me how you think your performance is going at the moment, please?'* However, if there's an issue with a specific piece of work or project, you could frame the question in relation to that. For example, an opening question could be: *'Can you tell me how you think your work on Project Sunshine is going, please?'*

Their response will be telling. They may be aware of the issue, and if so, they may or may not want to acknowledge it. However, you may also find that they don't feel anything is wrong. Your path to trying to address this through an informal approach depends on their response, as set out in the three options below.

1. They acknowledge all or part of the performance issue

This is a great start and means you can have a conversation that will enable you to increase your understanding, be curious and engage in an exploratory discussion. Depending on how they answer your opening question, you may want to ask a range of follow-up questions. My advice is to start by asking *'Are there circumstances I'm not aware of that you believe are contributing to this issue?*' If the answer is 'yes', you can then explore those circumstances and see what you can put in place to help, or what the individual needs to do or is already doing to address the relevant issue(s).

However, if the answer is 'no', then you may wish to reframe with a similar question, asking '*Can you think of any reason at all why there is this specific performance issue?*' Continuing in this vein can be helpful. However, if the individual can't explain why there's a problem, you may be best placed to take a lead on the discussion, sharing with them the performance problems in more detail and working through a range of possible causes to try to identify what is wrong. If no answer can be found, then I would suggest moving to solution mode and agreeing what steps need to be taken to ensure that the issue you're discussing doesn't persist.

It's worth remembering that sometimes the reasons for performance issues arise due to circumstances outside the workplace and that the individual may need support from other colleagues or professional help to tackle challenges they're facing.

2. They seem defensive but you suspect they may know there is a problem

Under these circumstances, it's best to stop exploring the individual's take on the issue, and to instead let them know that you have identified, or have been alerted to, an issue and would like to take the chance now to fully explore that, to hear their point of view and understand any circumstances that they think might be relevant to this matter.

It's essential, particularly when someone seems defensive, to demonstrate your impartiality, and just make clear that you're bringing an identified problem to discuss, but that you would like to get all the facts before any next steps are agreed.

Hopefully, by setting up this framing, it will enable a level of trust which allows you to list the main issues that have been identified, giving any evidence that you might have to support the claims. Be careful with how you outline the problem so as not to cause further defensiveness (such as using accusatory language) and be guided by the discussion that follows. If you think that the individual already knows there's an issue, you might want to indicate that through your questions.

To give you some examples, you could frame an issue as follows:

→ *'The report you produced for the finance team was returned to me as it had several errors in it, such as a table that referenced the incorrect year. This is the third month in a row this has happened, which we have discussed on prior occasions, so I know you are aware this has happened before. Why do you think this is still happening, please?'*

→ *'On more than one occasion, including in our planning meeting yesterday, I have observed you talking over your colleague Simone, interrupting them in meetings and dismissing their ideas. You seem uncomfortable when you do this, which makes me think you are aware this is happening. Is that the case, and do you see that this behaviour is causing difficulty? Is there an issue I need to be made aware of, please?'*

3. They seem to believe all is going well and are oblivious to the issues

This is the hardest response to tackle. The next steps and potential questions here are fairly similar to the ones above. You will need to emphasise that you want to understand the full issue and hear all the facts. However, you may need to be even more forthright in setting out the problem and detailing the evidence and remove any reference to suggestions that the individual is aware of the problem.

If, through discussion, the individual does not agree or

acknowledge the issue, despite setting out the evidence and information that has led you to this conclusion, and if they can't give you any rationale or explanation for circumstances which might be leading to the issues you have set out, then aside from setting out the actions you wish to see being delivered, you will need to explain that, despite their inability to agree there is a problem, if these issues continue it may lead to a more formal process.

In all three of these scenarios, remember that you are the person who will set the tone. Be calm, compassionate and clear. Do not shy away from discussing the problems as causing confusion to a colleague will not help to resolve the matter. This is why preparation is essential to ensure that you can be concise and articulate.

A final comment about performance management is that it's important as a leader to get the balance right between directing and giving autonomy. Once you have agreed a plan with your colleague, give them the freedom to get on with addressing the issues and keep an oversight of these matters through your regular meetings. If the issue continues to worsen, you will likely have no choice but to move to a more formal process. However, if someone responds well to the engagement, then give them the benefit of the doubt and a chance to address the matter. Your role is to encourage and ensure that you remove any barriers to their successful resolution of the issue.

Managing the process of removing an employee from an organisation

It's highly likely that you will, at some stage, have to work through a process of exiting an employee from an organisation. This might be because of changes to a team or company structure, which would mean going through a restructure or a redundancy consultation. In those circumstances, you should have HR help and will be able to follow a clear process.

A harder situation to deal with is having to ask someone to leave when the issue arises from them (and their work or behaviour) as opposed to circumstances beyond their control.

I have had to ask people to leave for a range of reasons, such as their professional behaviour, poor performance, because they have made an unacceptable error, or due to an inability or refusal to support the organisational strategic direction (with them acting as a blocker to progress).

I'm not going to cover the process here, as each organisation will have its own practice and guidance, and I'm not an HR expert. However, I have learnt some lessons over the years that I think would be useful to share.

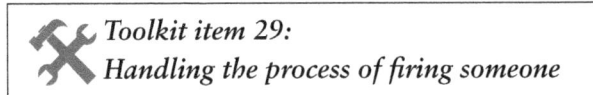

> **Toolkit item 29:**
> **Handling the process of firing someone**
>
> → **Act with kindness and compassion.** There's a need to be gentle in these circumstances. It's an unpleasant experience for both the employee affected and the line manager dealing with this issue. Think about how acting with kindness and compassion could be demonstrated. For example, do you need to have your conversation at your office, or near other staff, or can you meet elsewhere or online? Think about how you can offer support as they prepare to leave the organisation. You might also want to have a difficult conversation (particularly a 'without prejudice' discussion) in the morning to allow them to go home and process what has happened that afternoon.
> → **Minimise your emotional response.** These can be highly emotive situations. As much as you possibly can, do not react with emotion, no matter what is being said to you or how the person behaves. This is

different to protecting your wellbeing. If the impacted individual is overly aggressive, difficult or makes inappropriate accusations, you are within your rights to stop a conversation and say that the behaviour is not appropriate, and you will need to step away and come back to them regarding what will happen next.

→ **Work with HR colleagues.** Make sure you get advice, and if possible and appropriate, have an HR colleague in the room or on the call with you to ensure you follow company procedure and to protect you from a potential accusation of unfair treatment. When I've had an HR colleague in the discussion, I've tended to explain that they are there to capture an impartial record of what has been discussed.

→ **Having a 'without prejudice' discussion.** If you are going to do this, make sure you know what you need to do by engaging with HR colleagues or even an employment lawyer. These discussions take place when you want to speak bluntly about performance issues, and likely offer an alternative (usually an enhanced severance package) instead of a performance improvement process.

→ **Don't jump straight to a 'without prejudice' discussion.** If you know that you will likely end up needing to have this more formal discussion, it's worth trying to aim for as little animosity as possible. This can be achieved by exploring the extent to which the person you are talking to can understand the severity of the situation, as they may have been feeling that it's no longer tenable for them to deliver the performance or output required of their role. If that is the case, it can provide an opening for you to say to them that you want to ensure you agree a fair and confidential way for them to leave, and if they agree, that you would now like to move to a 'without prejudice' discussion.

> → **Be brave and direct.** No one likes doing this, but not directly articulating what you need to say will make the matter worse. Prepare fully, be ready with the points you want to make, listen and respond clearly, respect your colleague by engaging in eye contact if that's possible, and have courage. I've seen senior leaders being nervous or anxious in advance of these discussions – even managers who have been leading for many years – so know that you're not alone. But the best way through is the kindest, most direct route.

A useful book to refer to is Kim Scott's *Radical Candor* (2017), which describes what happens if you show you care personally for employees while also challenging them directly with 'clear, kind feedback that is not aggressive or insincere'.

Managing and dealing with effective meetings

What is an effective meeting?

An effective meeting has a few key components:

→ **A clear purpose,** so people understand why the meeting is happening and what it's aiming to achieve.
→ **The right people in attendance.** When inviting colleagues, it's wise to be clear who you are asking to attend because they are essential and who might find the meeting useful or provide some input but would be optional attendees.
→ **The right supporting information, reports and papers.** These need to be available sufficiently far in advance so colleagues get a chance to engage with them fully.
→ **A clear agenda,** which helps to manage expectations for the meeting. I like an agenda to include a table that lists each item in order:

Item	Description	Lead	Duration	Timing	Format and source info
Performance	Detailed review of Project Sunshine	JJ	30 mins	09:30–10:00	Presentation and group discussion
Finance	Detailed budget review by project area	FD	30 mins	10:00–10:30	Management accounts pack and finance director presentation

→ **A means to capture the output from the meeting.** This doesn't just have to be somebody taking minutes. If you don't have any support to do this, you could rotate the minute-taking among the attendees, film or record parts of the meeting or, in a workshop, take photos or screenshots of the output.

→ **Clear next steps.** This includes an action tracker, agreement on what needs to follow next and, ideally, a look ahead at what's coming up in future meetings so that staff can prepare in advance.

→ **An effective chair.** Somebody who will facilitate discussion, manage the input and ensure the meeting is kept to time. Timing is particularly important, as it's likely colleagues will have busy diaries, so over-running meetings will not help you or others.

Chairing meetings

Chairing a meeting is something you will get better at over time. As chair, your key role is to ensure that you're enabling the group to deliver on the output the meeting was set up to achieve. This may not always be straightforward. There are several leadership tactics you will likely need to deploy. Here are my hints and tips for you:

→ Ensure you have read the meeting papers and reports and be ready with thoughtful questions that will facilitate and prompt group discussion.
→ Ideally aim for your voice to be one of the least heard in the room or on the call. With each agenda item, it's helpful to set out what the item is looking to achieve, but then encourage others to contribute and lead relevant items.
→ Don't worry about periods of silence. Sometimes they can be effective in allowing colleagues to digest and reflect before giving input.
→ Be aware, particularly in hybrid meetings, of who wants to contribute and what their signals are. It's helpful to set out how participants will be able to engage – for example, if you're on a call that allows people to indicate by raising their hands – and you might want to request this etiquette for the meeting.
→ It's also helpful to recognise that in this age of hybrid meetings, some staff feel more comfortable contributing through the chat function rather than raising questions verbally. Chairing meetings in this new era has become more complicated, which is why preparation in advance is essential.

As an effective chair, you may need to influence a direction without being overly directive. My tool below helps with that challenge.

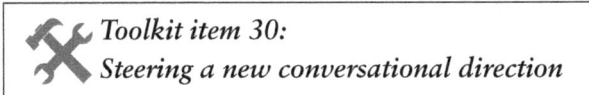

> *Toolkit item 30:*
> *Steering a new conversational direction*
>
> To change the conversation's direction without being too directive, I like to use a framing for asking questions that's fairly passive and encourages input. For example, try the following:

→ Swapping 'I think we should...' for 'Should we...?' or 'Would you be happy to...?'
→ Swapping 'I suggest the best thing to do would be to...' for 'What do the group think about...?'
→ Swapping 'We really must look at it this way' for 'Could we imagine what would happen if...?'

Chapter reflections

This chapter has explored a wide range of management relationships that you will lead, whether you're managing up, managing sideways or acting as a line manager. Management can be harder in some ways than leading and directing as it involves a two-way relationship, and you can only account for your own behaviours and actions; the other party's response is beyond your control. My aim has been to assist you with both the professional relationships you will have and then the wider responsibilities of management, from managing a team to dealing with underperformance, handling exiting someone from a company and managing effective meetings. I'm now going to move on to essential leadership skills that you might start to require as your journey unfolds.

6 Essential leadership skills

In designing this chapter, I reflected on the evolution of my own leadership journey beyond that first national role. As my roles grew in seniority and my accountabilities increased, I needed to develop further skills and identify tools that would help me. These included having the confidence to stand up for myself, to develop greater conviction that I knew what I was talking about and to start to help my team be more effective so that I could in turn be a more impactful leader. I also needed to consider what this heightened responsibility meant in terms of the toll it was taking on my wellbeing and stress levels. I hope the tools and frameworks here will help you as you further develop on your leadership path.

Before I share my essential leadership skills, I wanted to let you know about a fantastic book containing excellent hints and tips, which I read early in my career to assist me. This was Joseph Badaracco's *Leading Quietly* (2002), which talks about the fact that 'often the most effective leaders are rarely public heroes, they maintain a low profile, yet they do what is right (for themselves and their organisations) inconspicuously and without casualties'. This book provides a range of useful ways to lead, and I suggest you engage with it for further essential leadership skills.

Negotiation framework

Some women seem to struggle with negotiations. When I told a recruiter I worked with that I was writing this book, she implored me to include something about negotiation for women, as she shared that she finds it difficult that some women don't seem to be able to ask for or get what they deserve. She's not alone in thinking this. According to an article by Kim Elsesser in *Forbes* magazine (2021), referring to research published in the *Journal of Applied Psychology*, women can fall short in negotiations for two reasons. She talks about a 'tameness narrative', which essentially means that women struggle because they aren't sufficiently ambitious or assertive. She also goes on to suggest that women face 'a backlash' when they do negotiate assertively because people may not think it's appropriate for them to behave in this way.

I find this research interesting as it confirms what I have long been concerned about: for some, a woman being ambitious is perceived as a negative trait. I know other female leaders have had the same reaction.

I wanted to share some ideas about how to approach negotiation for the women who find this difficult so you can be successful in achieving the outcomes you desire.

Toolkit item 31: The negotiation toolkit

Preparing for negotiation

→ **What are the key points or point you wish to negotiate on?** Can you prepare your request to be as concise as possible and with as much clarity as you can give?

→ **Do your research in advance.** Having information to back up the rationale for your request is essential. For example, if you are negotiating on salary, are you aware of any benchmarking available on the role in comparable industries?

→ **Consider all the possible outcomes from the negotiation.** Be sure you know which you might accept and which would not deliver what you want.

→ **Aim for a win-win scenario.** What would that look like for you and for the person you are negotiating with? Start by thinking about the potential benefits your request or aims would have for the other party; it might be part of what you would wish to convey as you make your key points clearly and concisely.

During negotiation

→ **Be bold and brave.** Articulate exactly what you want (drawing on your preparation).

→ **Pay careful attention to how the conversation is unfolding.** You may have imagined or even rehearsed how the discussion might go, but it will rarely happen the way you think it will. Listen carefully and observe closely how your request is being received. You may continue to argue a point that you have already successfully won or you may realise that other avenues and solutions present themselves during the discussion which you hadn't considered before.

- → **Recognise when a 'no' means no (for now).** Aiming for a particular outcome and being offered something different, or being told that the answer to your request is 'no' or 'not right now', is not necessarily a failing. It might be that the conversation has revealed new possibilities you hadn't considered or it might be that there are wider circumstances at play of which you are unaware and a 'no' might be the best outcome for you.
- → **Have confidence in yourself.** Believe in the value you bring. Having this in your mind will help you to hold out for or make the best case for what you deserve.

After negotiation

- → **Reflect on what went well and what didn't.** If you didn't achieve your goal, it doesn't mean that it isn't something you couldn't revisit. It might be worth following up with the other party, thanking them for their consideration and asking whether there might be anything you could do in time to lead to a different outcome.
- → **Be proud of yourself.** Not everyone negotiates for what they want. Every time you do it, you will learn more about what works and be more capable in the future. As a leader, you will need a lot of resilience, and this is a good way to build that.

Remember, a negotiation often begins with a starting point, and what then follows is a strategic discussion where both parties will be assessing how they feel about what's being discussed, if they think it's fair, what they think the benefits are and what they are prepared to concede on or agree to. It's a process of going back and forth to ideally lead to a resolution of an issue in a way that you will both ultimately find acceptable. You may be negotiating on your salary. If that's the case, having done your research, there's no harm in starting off at the highest point you think would be fair, recognising that you're leaving yourself wiggle room to end up closer to a more realistic figure. Being clear in advance on the lowest acceptable value to you is an essential part of your negotiation preparation.

Trusting your gut

I thought it might be helpful to have some commentary on trusting your gut immediately following a section on negotiation. Sometimes you will need to be guided through a negotiation by gut instinct, and it's useful to consider why you might be able to trust this. Sarah Lloyd-Hughes, founder of Ginger Leadership Communications, asked me on a recent inspiring leadership development call what I meant by trusting my gut. I told her:

→ It's about recognising patterns of behaviour, indicators or warning signs and acknowledging when you feel that recognition, then looking to see what it is that you recognise and where you have experienced something similar in the past to help give you insights to assist with the present.
→ Over the years, you will undoubtedly have conducted your own internal lessons-learnt exercises, considering what has worked and what you could have done better. If you find yourself in a similar experience, you can be guided by that inner wisdom because you will have put the work in.
→ Trusting your gut is also about following your intuition. Sometimes you will have an inspiration or an idea but don't have all the evidence to back up why it might work. However, it feels like a risk worth taking. Taking

that risk, and continuing to do so, will help you to learn more about your intuition and will enable you to identify early warning signals when that gamble hasn't quite paid off, affording you the opportunity to correct the issue in time.

There's a lot of scientific analysis and evidence supporting the fact that we can hone and trust our gut instinct. Joel Pearson from the University of New South Wales describes this as your brain processing 'all the things in the environment' to draw a scientific conclusion and make a prediction 'based on prior learning, situations you've been in… all the things that you've been through in your life'. Pearson's book, *The Intuition Toolkit* (2024), describes this instinct as 'the learnt, positive use of unconscious information for better decisions or actions'.

The more you use your intuition and gut instinct, the more you hone this capability, giving you greater confidence to rely on it. It's a continuous improvement process. As one manager said to me, 'Jenny, why are you questioning this decision? You have the experience, which gives you the right to trust your gut instinct, and you should give it more weight than some of the counter arguments or evidence being presented.'

If I could say anything to anyone taking on a leadership role it would be to follow your own instincts. Having worked in the media industry for 22 years, starting at the very bottom, I'm 18 months into my biggest leadership role to date. I'm the first woman and the youngest person to take on the role, and while I've learnt a lot from those who've come before me, my best bit of advice would be: don't be afraid to do things differently. When I first got the job, I feared I wouldn't live up to my predecessors, but

I quickly realised that by leaning on my own strengths, I could create a more nurturing, inclusive and open team environment. A recent employee feedback report described my leadership style as modern and forward facing and highlighted how I've become a role model for many females working in more junior roles on the team.
Joanne, senior executive TV producer

Maintaining your wellbeing

Stress

This is one of the words I hear the most at work! We worry about stress levels, and generally use the term in a negative context; however, some level of stress is normal. It's nature's way of keeping us engaged and focused. An issue arises when stress tips from being acute to being chronic.

The source of your (or your team's) stress might be coming from the workplace and the current projects, tasks or challenges you're dealing with, but it can also come from many other sources. In short, stress results from dealing with demanding circumstances, some we can control and some we can't.

A helpful way to understand the stresses you're under, and to think about your coping mechanisms, is to use the 'stress bucket'. This is also a helpful exercise to do with your staff for their own learning and for you to gain insight into how they are coping and what mechanisms work for them.

Toolkit item 32: The stress bucket

The stress bucket is a container. Stress from all different sources pours in. A problem occurs when there's too much stress and the container overflows. To help ourselves, we need to develop coping strategies, which are essentially a valve or tap to release stress from the bucket.

→ **Step 1** – Complete an exercise to consider what's in your stress bucket and what your current coping strategies are. If you like, draw a bucket and add all your stresses into it, then set out the different coping strategies you apply underneath your tap.

→ **Step 2** – Draw a circle around the stresses you can control and put a cross over the ones that are outside your control.

→ **Step 3** – Consider if your bucket is mainly stresses you can or can't control. What does that tell you? Where you can control stresses, ask yourself if you're

Essential leadership skills

> taking all the necessary actions you can to manage those stresses. If not, what one action might you take to reduce or remove one of those stressors?
> → **Step 4** – Test whether you have proportionate and sufficient coping strategies in place for the level and number of stresses you experience. A full bucket with one stress release is not enough!
>
> My further tips:
>
> → Try to identify the physical, psychological and behavioural tells or signs you show when you're feeling stressed or overwhelmed. This might help you to see how stress impacts you in different ways.
> → You can do the above steps as a team exercise, too. You might want to encourage colleagues to recommend coping mechanisms that work for them to share with others.

?

→ Have you drawn your stress bucket?
→ Can you see ways in which you can act on a stressor to reduce or remove it?
→ Would you feel comfortable sharing your bucket, coping mechanisms and telltale signs with your manager to enhance their understanding of how to best support you?

Coping mechanisms

A coach once asked me how I have so much drive and energy with a stressful job, and my (half joking) answer was that it's something I seriously invest a lot of time, energy and a proportion of my salary into. I feel that being well and maintaining a healthy balance is essential, given my demands as a leader. Here are some steps you might consider:

Establish a great daily routine

How you start the day sets the tone for the rest of it. Do you have a moment of calm before you get going? Do you exercise first thing or do some stretching? When you get up, do you make your bed and feel as if your house is in order before you start work? It's worth thinking about your day ahead: what will it entail and what do you want to achieve?

At the end of the day, make sure you wind down before going to sleep. It may be that you have work matters on your mind. If so, you could write them down so those whirring thoughts can be transferred from your head to paper to be picked back up the next morning. I find that this aids my sleep.

Avoid burnout

It's tempting to fit in all the social occasions and invitations you get, alongside other commitments, friends, family and, of course, your work. However, be wary of burnout. Sometimes, something has got to give, and I would urge you to put your wellbeing first, and remember that it's OK, and even empowering, to say 'no' sometimes. People will understand.

Find out what gives you joy and fit it in!

My list of essential activities or experiences I must do on a regular basis to ensure that I maintain my mental wellbeing include:

- → exercise
- → learning
- → being out in nature
- → relaxing – reading or watching a favourite programme
- → moving at least one thing forward (not feeling I have a stagnant 'to do' list that is not progressing)

The basics for wellbeing

My online fitness coach Kasey shares that wellbeing basics include:

→ drinking plenty of water
→ movement – whatever works for you, even if it's simply walking
→ eating a nutritious diet most of the time
→ getting good sleep
→ maintaining a tracker that notes the above four items, which can help you keep an eye on how you're doing.

Leading change

Adaptation is a key leadership skill, as is the ability to draw on your resilience to handle the challenges in front of you. As a leader, you need to lead your team in a way that enables them to manage challenges in a flexible, creative, agile and robust way.

I haven't come across a brilliant toolkit or framework that you can apply on the spot when faced with adversity or difficulty. Instead, for me, preparation is everything. This means ensuring that your team have the skills, mindset and capabilities to respond with agility and resilience when needed. My adaptability and resilience framework aims to help you cultivate these qualities.

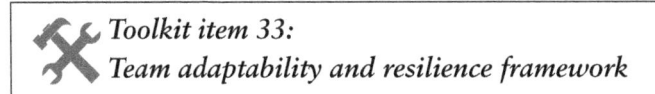

> *Toolkit item 33:*
> *Team adaptability and resilience framework*
>
> **Learning, development and self-care**
> Investigate developmental support options to help with adaptation and resilience, such as courses, reading and training on versatility, vulnerability, handling conflict, decision making, strategy in practice, operations strategy

and other subjects. On the less formal side, demonstrating a care for staff wellbeing will help colleagues feel supported and will in turn create a safe space for them to test their limits and explore solutions to problems. Staff knowing that you will support them no matter the circumstances will encourage people to be more open to risk and be able to respond effectively to overcome challenges when they come along.

Conduct lessons-learnt exercises
These are useful to help staff understand the root causes of any failures, to be impartial and to not assign blame, so that the learning will help refine their approach for the future. It's important that these are conducted to look at the problem objectively and that staff feel there's a safe space for this review. Demonstrate your own adaptability by being open to feedback and showcasing a willingness to learn from successes and failures.

Help staff feel comfortable with change
This is an important role that a leader can play. Emphasising the positive benefits of change is essential, as is having a clear vision that staff can engage with and support. I recently read a great book by Kotter and Rathgeber called *Our Iceberg is Melting* (2005), which is a fantastic way to explain change. I would advise a leader to not only read it themselves but also encourage their team to read it, as it is a short but charming tale that helps explain the importance of acting to stay relevant and successful.

Empower staff
Staff need to feel empowered to make decisions in difficult circumstances. If they're not used to this, when problems strike, they may feel helpless and unable to respond. Using the decision-making framework in this

Essential leadership skills

book (pages 78–81) will help to determine when and if this is appropriate. If it is, then giving your team input into matters that affect them or where they have expertise will ensure that problems are more likely to be mitigated and staff feel a greater sense of control and ownership.

Scenario response planning
This not only helps staff to work through what they might need to do when faced with a business issue, but will also enable them to feel they have some control in circumstances which might be problematic or chaotic. Working through scenarios helps staff know how to respond and how to use the available tools and processes when needed.

Positive reinforcement
Take the time to acknowledge the small victories achieved by your staff as this will help them recognise when they're using the appropriate skills and tools and when they're applying the mindset that will be needed in times of challenge. It will also reinforce a belief that they can be adaptable and resilient, and this competence will help build a sense of confidence.

Act as a role model
Demonstrating how you can adapt your own style will help encourage staff. This might include seeking out feedback about how you're performing, asking colleagues to share what they thought went well and what could be improved about an initiative you have led, and then making changes in response and sharing that with the team. This will show your willingness to learn and embrace change.

Problem solving and creativity

Leaders spend a lot of time solving problems. I have found these steps effective with a team.

> **Toolkit item 34:**
> **Problem-solving steps**
>
> → Examine the problem – articulate it and agree a problem statement with the team.
> → Get as much information (feedback, evidence, data) as possible to help understand the problem you have set out.
> → Come up with questions you want to answer about the problem and, when you have agreed a list, work with your team to explore ideas to generate possible answers. Be as expansive as possible, and do not judge ideas or dismiss them. Make sure you capture everything possible.
> → Try to come up with a solution to the problems based on the ideas you have heard, considering which is the best fit for the problem statement. Make sure you evaluate all your options and remember it may be that a combination of solutions is the answer rather than just one.
> → Agree a plan to address the issue with clear accountabilities and timescales.

Sometimes it isn't possible to resolve an issue using the tried and tested methods you might ordinarily apply. This is where creativity comes in. If you can find new ways to examine problems, it will help you and your team gain confidence that you can come up with a solution.

I have a few approaches I like to apply when problem

Essential leadership skills

solving. Before I talk about those in more detail, I wanted to share some learning that has helped me in working through problem solving with a team.

> **Toolkit item 35:**
> **Team vulnerability to aid problem solving**
>
> I read about an exercise where three groups were asked to solve a problem.
>
> → Group 1 were told there were no wrong answers.
> → Group 2 were told there were wrong answers and that's OK, that the team should constructively challenge and build on ideas to get to better answers.
> → Group 3 were asked to share something personal about themselves before they started the problem-solving exercise (remember I always say you should only share as much as you are comfortable with sharing).
>
> Group 1 had a fairly successful meeting and came up with some good output.
>
> Group 2 had even better results and a higher quality of answers.
>
> Group 3 were the most successful, being able to feed back, critique and be kind and open to sharing ideas because vulnerability was established and trust was built.
>
> This is one reason why I encourage management teams to share a personal insight each week, as over the years that builds closeness and trust.

My preferred go-to creative problem-solving techniques

Reverse brainstorming

Brainstorming is when you come up with all possible ideas to find a solution to a problem. Reverse brainstorming gets you to come up with all the ways in which you can make the problem worse. By doing this first (which can be fun and cathartic), you can then start to fill in the right-hand column with the opposite answer. This can generate new and different ideas to solve the problem that might not be identified by standard brainstorming.

For example: 'We are not keeping our funder happy, and it seems the relationship is rather negative.'

Worst case (make it worse)	Reverse
Never turn up to meetings on time	Always arrive early and well prepared
Do not fulfil KPIs and performance targets	Meet or even exceed targets
Do not respond to requests for information	Actively seek out whether case studies, data or other input might be needed and helpful

SCAMPER

This is a method for asking questions to spark creative thinking. The acronym and suggested questions are:

→ S – Substitute: what could I replace that might lead to success?
→ C – Combine: how could I combine elements to make a difference?
→ A – Adapt: what could I change to enable me to

address this problem in a new way?
→ M – Magnify: what elements could I expand or boost to make a difference?
→ P – Put to other uses: how could I use other products or services, people, tools or frameworks to have an impact?
→ E – Eliminate: what could I take out that could help?
→ R – Rearrange: how can I change this situation? what are my options to reframe or reorder this situation?

Attribute listing

A good example that emphasises why attribute listing is useful is the famous NASA attempt to develop pens that would write in space. If they had considered the attributes of the problem they were trying to solve, they might have more quickly identified their end solution (after spending a lot of money on R&D) – a pencil!

Attribute listing is a structured way to approach problem solving. It involves taking complex problems and breaking them down into their individual attributes, enabling you to examine each attribute in isolation.

This allows you to do several things. You may identify possible new uses for those attributes to apply now or use later as part of other solutions. You might be able to use the SCAMPER model to consider substituting or taking out an attribute and seeing if that would make a difference, or you might recombine the attributes in innovative ways.

As part of applying different techniques to solve problems, it's important to encourage a culture where innovation is valued.

> Value innovation – women can offer valuable perspectives and approaches to the ideation process that can result in more innovative solutions to complex problems, so don't hold back. Exploring different viewpoints and insights can enable more effective problem solving that can lead to greater strategic alignment within a team and organisation.
> *Amanda Foreshaw, HR lead, strategic business partner and leadership coach*

Understanding cultural intelligence

I believe leaders must ensure they understand enough about and consider equity, diversity, inclusion and belonging in their work. It's important that you have the skills, confidence and capabilities to respond and act appropriately. You must lead on acknowledging the many benefits of cultural diversity, recognise the challenges of achieving inclusion, take an active stance in speaking out about these issues and understand the absolute necessity to act with fairness to create workplaces where everyone can belong. I'm fortunate to have a peer and friend who is an expert on cultural intelligence, so I'm sharing a detailed update from her in the hope that this will enhance your understanding and inspire you with some self-reflection questions.

> Charles Darwin emphasised the importance of adaptability as the key to survival.
> Adaptability is at the heart of cultural intelligence. In

my work, I often need to explain that cultural intelligence is more than understanding how people from different nationalities can work together. It's about every aspect (the food we eat, customs we celebrate, places we visit, our gender, religion, nationality, ethnicity) that we identify with, which forms part of who we are.

Cultural intelligence is relevant to organisational culture and is defined as our ability to work with people who are different to us. Specifically, the capability to function and relate effectively in culturally diverse situations.

Cultural intelligence/quotient, or 'CQ', is formed of four capabilities. These are:

→ CQ drive – your level of interest, persistence and confidence during multicultural interactions. Your 'why' driver that makes you want to consider and be motivated to work with and understand people who are different to you, and your level of self-confidence in doing that.

→ CQ knowledge – your level of understanding regarding how cultures are similar or different. This is informed by the books you read, the social media you engage with, the podcasts you listen to, the conversations you have and the policies and procedures you adopt.

→ CQ strategy – your awareness and ability to plan for multicultural interactions. Are you observing what's going on in the interactions happening in front of you? Can you flex, and adapt and respond to the differences that arise from that engagement? Do you check whether the interaction went well and, where it didn't, think about what needs to be adapted? It's about taking your CQ knowledge and CQ drive and applying that strategically.

→ CQ action – your ability to adapt when working in a multicultural context. It's how you show up in those interactions with people who are different from you:

when do you adapt, when do you not? It's a reflection of the decisions you take.

It's a skill we can and must all develop if we want to be effective leaders in a diverse, digital and divided world. We can do this because:

→ CQ drive is about motivating yourself, which we can all do.
→ CQ knowledge is how you learn about cultures you interact with and we can all engage in learning and understanding.
→ CQ strategy is about how you prepare in order to anticipate and adjust to interactions.
→ CQ action is how you use adaptation skills.

As leaders we can develop CQ through our experiences, by taking chances to reflect, where necessary, to sit with discomfort and put ourselves in situations not familiar to us, since we must recognise that it's easier for us to work with people like us than those who are different to us.

Remember that whatever gets us to a point of understanding will not keep us there, and we need to keep updating our skills and knowledge to continue to make a difference.

Ritika Wadhwa, CEO and founder, Prabhaav Global

My learning from interactions with thought leaders on this topic is that you must seek out answers yourself and not expect others, especially those who represent a minority, to educate you.

?

How well informed and confident do you feel about cultural intelligence and addressing inclusion and belonging in the workplace? Where can you find out more?

Tools for team reflection and assessment

Encouraging your team to reflect and assess how well they are performing will help you to ensure the team keeps improving.

Team effectiveness

I designed a quick spreadsheet tool to assess team effectiveness, which I asked each member to fill in, scoring both themselves and their colleagues. It was helpful for me as a manager to understand the self-assessment of my staff and the perceptions of their teammates, and to identify areas for development to ensure maximum team effectiveness.

> **Toolkit item 36:**
> **Team contribution assessment tool**

To what extent do you/ your colleague:	Score yourself in this column	Score for Colleague A	Score for Colleague B
Make contributions that develop a discussion?			
Create a sense of excitement and momentum about work?			
Provide constructive challenge?			
Provide new input or perspectives to reframe an issue?			
Bring innovative thinking to the team?			

In each column score from 1 (low) to 5 (high).

Real Deal cards

Another method I like to apply to understand my team is Dr Paul Stolz's Real Deal cards. These are produced by PEAK Learning and are a tactile and highly effective communication tool.

The pack contains words and phrases covering aspects that matter to you in a workplace, such as 'Being heard', 'Offering insights', 'Honesty', 'Making a difference' and 'Sense of purpose'.

A good way to engage with the pack is to ask staff to go as quickly as possible through the cards and select the ones that matter to them. Then narrow that selection to five cards and choose one that is the dealbreaker – the aspect that would be a red line and if crossed or disrespected, might well cause them to resign.

Doing this is highly effective: first, you know exactly what matters to people, so you can focus your energies on that aspect to engage them; second, you can share your team profile, so your team can all know each other better; third, you can track how what matters most changes. With one team we did this every year for three years and it was helpful to see what changed and discuss why.

Team check-in

A useful method for team reflection is to go round and get one or two words from everyone as a temperature check on how they are feeling and ask them to explain why. Although this is hardly groundbreaking, as a leader it's helpful to check the mood of the group.

Imagine you're about to launch into a new project but you hear from your team that many of them are stressed and dealing with complex issues outside work. You might then want to adjust your tone or approach. Or if you find out that everyone is feeling buoyed up and they are ready to tackle the problem, you might alter the item you want to cover and make the best use of that energy.

Essential leadership skills

Helpful tool for team development days

I have designed a number of different team or company away days over the years and have attended just as many designed and facilitated by others. Bringing your team together (in person is best, but online may be necessary) is a valuable way to connect, undergo some learning, ensure that everyone is on the same page with direction and objectives, undertake problem-solving activities or get creative on a new product or initiative.

There may be other reasons you might wish to bring colleagues together, so before you book an away day, think about the main aim. It can help to consider how you want people to feel afterwards and what you would like them to have understood or know.

> **Toolkit item 37:**
> **Away day design framework**
>
> I started designing away days by asking myself: what would I like my colleagues to think, feel, be and do?

What would I like my colleagues to:	Considerations	Activity ideas
Think?	This could include a range of areas. You might want the 'thinking' part of the agenda to be about something that's connected to team goals, performance, objectives or strategy. You may wish to focus on how your team delivers the company vision and mission.	• You could try reverse brainstorming to address a strategic issue. • You could take the mission or vision and break down the key words, then consider your team's role in fulfilling that aspiration.

Feel?	This really depends on the circumstances your team is facing. If you're trying to galvanise enthusiasm or support for an initiative or a strategy, you might be aiming for them to feel enthused and excited. If you're using the time to address how you move away from a difficult period, you may want them to feel hopeful.	• This 'feeling' element is a nice chance to get creative. In one company, I provided craft materials and asked staff to construct a future vision of a workspace relevant to our sector. • You may feel there's a need to engage in some trust-building exercises or ask people to share how they're feeling with a team check-in. • Perhaps you could discuss a 'team stress bucket' and agree some collective coping mechanisms.
Be?	This is where I link to work on culture, values, behaviour, organisational brand or vision.	• A nice exercise to do here is to work on the company values and consider how they apply to your team. How does your team demonstrate and deliver on the 'trust' value, for example? • Another fun exercise is to think about how you are perceived from an external lens and to create posters or brand concepts linked to what your team produces.

Do?	This is where you aim to encourage others to act following the session you have run.	• You could create a team commitment as a group, or you could also ask individual members to reflect and think about what they would do or how they would respond differently given what you have covered on the day.

Once you have considered these questions, you're ready to design a plan and form an agenda for your day. As the architect of the session, remember to include not just what an agenda item is, but state what the success criteria will be (what will good look like?) and how that agenda item will happen (will it be through a workshop, will there be a presentation, will you ask others to facilitate a session?). You may want an external speaker or trainer, particularly if you want to fit some learning and development into the day. Plan sufficient time for each item, including giving out any instructions, allowing time for people to do the tasks or exercises and for feedback (this always takes longer than you think!).

Chapter reflections

I hope you now have greater confidence in yourself and your ability to lead your team and feel ready to handle any leadership challenge that comes your way. If you have a team day coming up, will you try using the four questions to help you design that interaction? Perhaps you might try some of my favourite problem-solving techniques on your next challenge. The next chapter shares some insights about what it means to lead in the context of the wider organisation to help you consider that broader lens.

7 Your role in the context of organisational leadership

When I first started in leadership positions, I wasn't working closely with the senior leadership team and it seemed to me a bit of a mystery how the whole organisation was run effectively and what their accountabilities or responsibilities were. In fact, as my peer, Martin, said to me recently about their first senior role, 'At that time, I probably only thought the CEO was the "leader".' This is a useful reminder that new leaders may have this perception, but as many come to learn, it's not just about one individual – it takes a great team!

As for me, it's unlikely that your first leadership role will be one that sits in that top team. However, as you're part of the wider leadership team for the whole organisation, it's important to understand the organisational approach and strategy and then reflect that through your own team direction.

It's also helpful to observe and learn from the leaders in your organisation, as Rachel shares:

> I have always found it helpful to be curious and keen to learn from everyone. Watching, thinking and, when

possible, asking. Consider what you like or don't like about the leadership style of people, be it seniors, peers or others. There is always something that can help shape the kind of leader you want to authentically be. It's easier than trying to be someone else!
Rachel Musson, founder of Positively Resourceful Ltd

Organisational development stages and what they mean for leadership

Although you won't have full accountability for impacting on some of what you read here, it's helpful to appreciate the wider organisational leadership challenges that might be faced based on the evolution and stage of your company's development.

To do this, I want to use a concept called an organisational life cycle. This is a helpful but simple way of thinking about the company development stage in a format that looks a little like an 'S', which is why it is called the 'S curve'. This method was used to consider long-term economic cycles (Kondratiev 1925), and it was Richard Foster of McKinsey who then developed the tech/innovation model (1986). From these beginnings, the use has since been adapted, mainly for product or service life cycles. However, I personally find it helpful to apply when thinking about an organisation's evolution.

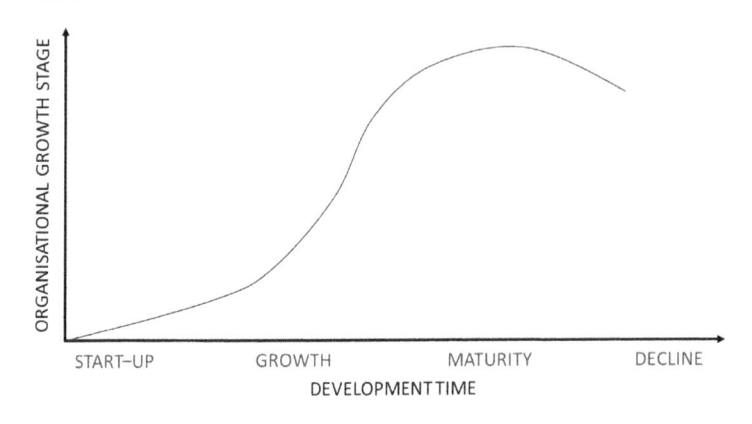

The S curve and organisational growth stages

In this model, as applied to an organisation, the growth stages can be considered as follows:

→ **Start-up.** This is the beginning point for an organisation or new company. At this early stage, the organisation will be finding its way, potentially still developing products or services. It's likely to have a smaller headcount than it will do ultimately and may be in an exploratory development stage. It's unlikely to have fully effective systems for operating, and the organisation will be in the process of establishing its culture and ways of working.

A key remit for the SLT at this stage will be considering how its products or services satisfy the customers in the markets in which the organisation is operating. It's likely that any funding has come from a founder, from an organisation that sets up a new company as part of its portfolio, from public or private investors, or because the organisation has won funding in the form of a grant or contract.

→ **Growth.** Organisations at this stage are evolving beyond the early phase, although growth might not really kick in for some time. In a growth phase, the organisation is becoming clearer on its purpose and will have established a customer base and stakeholders who benefit from its services or products. Unlike the start-up phase, when everything is probably more emergent, in this phase, the organisation will grow in a more planned and strategic way. Roles and responsibilities should be more clearly defined.

A key remit for the SLT will be to determine the goal or objective that drives growth. It might be in profit, headcount, turnover, the number of products or services the organisation offers, its locations, reach or reputation. It's likely that more than one of these things will be a focus at the same time.

→ **Maturity.** Not all companies reach maturity and stay there in a stable way. Some never quite get there and their growth fizzles out. Some might reach maturity, seemingly plateau, but then enter a further growth phase rather than starting a decline.

A key remit for the SLT will be considering how to transition towards stability, maximise income and improve the bottom line. It's likely that stability will lead to greater efficiencies than during the growth phase.

→ **Decline.** This can happen for lots of reasons. A company might be set up for a specific purpose, and when that need is met, the company closes. It could be that the company is not able to bring in profits to sufficiently cover its costs or debts, resulting in a winding up of the business, a sale or a declaration of bankruptcy. Some declines are caused by a significant change in customer demand or expectation as new technology emerges (think Blockbuster Video).

A key remit for the SLT will be to think about how best to wind the company down and how to keep the necessary employees who need to be involved until the end (that is if there's a planned and known endpoint). However, if the company is trying to remedy a decline, the team might do all they can to stay afloat. This could include cutting costs, focusing on core business and selling assets. If this attempt to resolve issues isn't managed well, it can speed up the pace of the decline rather than slow it.

Your role in organisational leadership

?

→ What stage in the S curve is your company at?
→ What about any other companies you have worked in?
→ What are the implications of the development stage and what challenges do you think it brings for the SLT and leaders of the company?

Being part of an SLT

For ease of reference, I use SLT in this book, but a top team might be called something different. In some organisations it's the senior management team (SMT), in others the executive or the corporate leadership team.

I wanted to briefly examine here the difference between being in the team that's accountable for the leadership and running of an organisation – and leading a team *within* that organisation. While there may be aspects of an organisation's delivery and success that an individual team is accountable for, the overall most senior leadership team has the collective accountability for all component parts and for delivering the strategy agreed with the governing body. It also has other legal accountabilities, such as producing the company's financial annual statement and accounts.

The SLT will have responsibility for managing downwards and leading and overseeing the organisation, its governance, its frameworks, ways of working, the culture and the delivery of the strategy. That team will also be responsible for managing upwards and outwards. This includes managing and meeting the expectations of the governing body and managing the expectations of and relationships with external stakeholders.

If you get to spend time with the SLT, use it as a learning experience. A previous colleague of mine had some invaluable advice:

Get yourself into rooms where senior people are doing their work as early and as often as possible. I didn't understand the context well where I first became a leader until I had witnessed first hand those above me – not just what they said, but what they asked about, what they cared about, who they listened to, what they worried about, were sincere about and what they were cynical about.
David Russell, senior director, government relations UK, Pearson

The organisation's operating manual

These are the key frameworks, tools, processes and ways of working that companies have in place to enable successful leadership, management and delivery. This section explores what's in the organisation's operating manual and considers what your actions should be as a leader in relation to these elements:

→ **A strategy.** Most companies have a published strategy document. This sets out the vision and mission of the organisation, what you're aiming to achieve and how you're going to get there.

Your leadership action: As a leader, it's important to understand this strategy, to ensure you're up to speed with the intended direction and that your team is geared up to be effective at delivering what the organisation is aiming to achieve.

→ **A leader.** This may be a CEO, MD or founder. Whatever the title, a company needs to have someone who is overarchingly accountable for its success.

Your leadership action: If you can, get to know your company leader. What drives them, how do they make decisions, what is their background? This is useful for times when you might interact with them and helps you understand how the organisation could develop under their stewardship.

→ **Mission statement.** This sets out the company's core values and purpose. It's usually a concise phrase, which generally articulates what the company does, how it does it and why.

Your leadership action: It's useful to be guided by the mission statement when reflecting on your objectives, what your team is delivering and how aligned your work is with the organisation's purpose.

→ **Vision statement.** A statement that describes the goals and ambitions of your company. It distils your company's vision for the future in a way that's memorable, pithy and can serve as a guide or even be a mantra to inspire colleagues.

Your leadership action: Make use of this emotive statement to inspire your team to work towards the objectives of the company. This is helpful when you're dealing with challenging times when you might need to rally your staff.

→ **Company finances.** Your organisation will have various sources of funds, which are essential to enable the company to operate. Without finance, you cannot function.

Your leadership action: It's crucial to understand your company finances. Where does the funding come from? Does your team contribute to generating income for the organisation? How much is in the company reserves that might be spent on improvement projects for the organisation? Being informed about your finances is as important as being informed about strategy.

→ **Staff/employees.** Staff are needed to perform the duties and activities that fulfil the company's mission and vision.

Your leadership action: Understanding the organisational structure and composition of the workforce is helpful. Does the company employ everybody full time or have a mixture of contractors, fixed term and permanent staff? What is expected of you as a leader in terms of how you design your team?

→ **Values.** It would be unusual to work somewhere without a defined set of values. These are intended to reflect both internally and externally what matters most to the organisation in terms of how it operates, its reputation and how it will engage with others.

Your leadership action: Make sure you embrace the values and use them to set the standards for how you and your team operate. Find out how the company uses the values. Is there an expectation that they frame how you work, how you assess staff performance, how you approach projects?

→ **Operating frameworks, processes and procedures.** Depending on its organisational development stage (page 174), your company should have at least some operating processes, procedures and frameworks. These set out how the organisation should be run and form the source documentation regarding ways of working to enable staff to have clarity on how they need to operate.

Your leadership action: Make sure you understand the expected operating approach and engage with those processes and procedures.

→ **Controls.** A company will need to have controls in place. These are the checks and balances, risk-mitigation elements, staff with the responsibility to protect the organisation, automated mechanisms that ensure there is organisational compliance or appropriate restrictions and limitations that prevent fraud and open the company to risk.

Your leadership action: It is of paramount importance that you work within the organisational controls. Failing to do so could result in disciplinary action or potentially even being asked to leave the organisation. It's also your responsibility as a manager to ensure that your team adheres to the organisation's controls. Get help from HR if you find this is not the case.

When I was designing an approach to leading a new directorate in my early thirties and wanted to convey how a team needed to operate with all the necessary instructions, direction and procedures, I realised that a car was a great way to frame this. Visualising driving a company car is a simple method for remembering the elements needed and understanding their purpose!

Toolkit item 38: The organisational operating manual – the company car

Operating manual items	Our company car
Strategy	Acts as the navigation system, helps you know where to go and how you are going to get there.
Leader	Sitting in the driver's seat. You want one person steering and controlling the acceleration, as multiple drivers could cause issues with directions and speed control. However, if you are a distributed leader or servant leader (see page 11), it's likely that as a driver, your route and speedometer will be influenced by the SLT.
Mission and vision statement	The exterior of the car, the look and feel, the colour, the brand. Essentially, how you present yourself to both passengers and passers-by.
Company finances	The wheels of your car. They need to keep spinning. If they stop, so do you!
Staff	The passengers. Some may be back seat drivers, some are asking 'Are we there yet?', some are distracted by the scenery, some are enjoying the drive, some may ask you to stop the car so they can get out.
Values	How you drive. Fast? Safely? With consideration? With the comfort and safety of your passengers in mind? Economically to save fuel?
Operating framework, processes and procedures	The instruction manual in the glovebox: you will need to refer to this to understand how the company operates.
Controls	The brakes, safety measures and airbags. Controls help prevent the car from skidding off the road and crashing.

Considering challenges at different levels of the organisation

A useful approach for considering organisational ways of working and operational effectiveness is organisational behaviour (OB), a discipline that looks at a company on multiple levels and draws on principles from psychology, sociology and anthropology. There are different ways that OB specialists analyse an organisation. Some consider three main levels of analysis: micro (individuals), meso (groups) and macro (the organisation). However, when I studied at Warwick Business School, we looked at a fourth level: societal impact.

Taking the four lenses that Warwick applied, I wanted to share how I use these in considering organisational challenges through the model below.

> **Toolkit item 39:**
> **Levels of organisational analysis – the SOGI model**
>
> When considering an issue, ask yourself how it might be manifesting or impacting at all these levels.
>
> S – Societal level
> O – Organisational level
> G – Group level (could be division, team or department level)
> I – Individual level

A practical example of this is to consider a scenario where you have heard that there's a staff member who is unhappy with their salary.

→ If you only look at the individual level, you might think this is just one disgruntled employee.
→ If you look at the team level, you may find they're not

the only person who feels this way.
→ If you take it to an organisational level, you might be assessing whether there have been changes in your organisation that might be driving dissatisfaction, such as a restructure. It could be that roles have substantially altered in scope or workload but no salary review accompanied the change.
→ If you take it up a level again and consider the macro-level factors, it might be that there is a cost of living crisis or high levels of inflation, and staff within that group, at that salary level, are particularly impacted.

You can see that if you look at the problem at all four levels, there may be adjustments that need to be made without just assuming that one individual employee is disgruntled.

Organisational values and culture

Values are an essential part of the organisational operating manual and companies can use them in a range of ways. At one end of the scale, they can simply be a brand exercise and not really something that staff reflect on or use in terms of how they interact with others. This can cause challenges if there's a difference between how the company says it operates and how it behaves.

On the other, more positive end of the spectrum, a company may have a set of values that are fully evident across all ways of working, are embodied by leaders and staff members, and form part of the reputation of the organisation. When there is strong alignment and cohesion between how a company says it operates and how it behaves, this creates high levels of trust and engagement.

As a leader, you can use organisational values in a range of ways:

→ **To reflect on team effectiveness.** I like to use values in important meetings or lessons-learnt activities to test whether or not we have behaved in line with how we wish to operate.

→ **To assess performance of staff**, using performance reviews to consider not just whether the colleague has fulfilled expectations in terms of deliverables and hit their objectives, but also to think about how they undertook that work and whether that was aligned with how the organisation wants to operate.

→ **Through staff recognition.** I like to give out awards to colleagues to celebrate when they have demonstrated what we're hoping to achieve through the values.

→ **To highlight any inappropriate or incorrect practice.** Values are a helpful mirror to hold up to help staff reflect on whether they have treated another colleague, or an external partner, in a way which does not match with the organisation's desired way of working.

→ **As part of promotional material to demonstrate how you work.** Particularly when you're considering how you might attract new colleagues to the organisation. When I was running a previous company, I felt huge pride that staff not only knew about our values (that I had led the design of) but that they chose to join the company because of them. At that time, our values were a key reason why we achieved number two best company to work for among the not-for-profit bodies in the UK and the number six mid-sized company in the whole of London in the Best Companies assessment.

It's most likely that the organisation you join already has values and ways in which it uses them. As a leader, you'll need to make sure you understand how you're expected to apply the values through your work. If the organisation is not currently using the suggestions above, it might be something you would like to recommend.

Chapter reflections

This chapter has lifted the analysis and insight from your leadership role to thinking about how you lead in the context of the wider organisation. It's intended as a stepping stone to a future, more senior role. Do you hope that one day you will be accountable for the organisational leadership we have reflected on here? Would you like to drive the 'company car'? Or be accountable for the company response to the development position on the S curve? Would you like it if staff joined your company because they felt you and your colleagues championed your values? I hope so, and I would be thrilled if this book is part of what helps to get you there.

8 How your manager can help you

Having buy-in from your manager, and somebody who believes in you, is essential to help address the issue of a lack of belief in female leadership. So I have written this final chapter to assist you with getting that support from your organisation's leaders and managers.

You could engage with this in a range of ways. You might want to share with your manager and let them know which questions it would be useful to explore together. You may feel comfortable giving them the whole chapter to read or you may want to keep this to yourself, but use it when you want to address a particular issue. How you engage with your manager will depend on their personality and on your relationship.

> **Toolkit item 40:**
> **Engaging your manager in supporting you**
>
> **If you feel supported already and feel comfortable...** you could give your manager a copy of this book and ask them to look through it, particularly concentrating on this last section, so that they can be helped to see things from the perspective of somebody going through the experience of being a new female leader.
>
> **If asking a manager to read this book is too much...** you may want to just share the table in this section to work through together.
>
> **If you don't feel comfortable in sharing the content of this book at all...** you can use the guidance and reflection questions below and frame them to address the specific issues in the chapters that have arisen for you. For example, if you felt that you wanted help with leading a new initiative, you could review the questions in that section of Chapter 2, form your own conclusions and ask your manager if they would be open to testing some of your queries and analysis on the initiative, given their leadership experience. Or you could take the questions here and put them to your manager in a way that engages their input. One example could be: *'I have been reflecting on my leadership style and feel that I am operating as a supportive leader. Would you agree with my assessment, and would you be able to share how you frame your style so I can understand better how you like to lead?'*

The following table breaks down each chapter with guidance and reflection questions for supporting a female leader through her journey.

Chapter and theme	Guidance/reflection questions
1. Establishing yourself as a leader	• How could you support female leaders in their exploration of leadership styles? This could include sharing more about your own style and then feeding back which style you see your employee demonstrating. • Can you give any guidance as to whether the style they operate is fit for purpose for the organisation and their remit? • If your organisation or your female leader's team are handling a crisis and they had to adopt a command and control approach, could you support your staff with how to adopt this (potentially less comfortable) leadership style? • Does your female leader have a coach, mentor or ambassador? If not, does your organisation operate a scheme which could enable them to find this support? • Would you be a good mentor to one or more of your female employees?
2. Leadership in practice	• How much experience does your employee have in leading a team? How could you support them with this? • If your employee is leading a significant initiative, could you work through some of the questions in Chapter 2 of this book and help them with the considerations, so that they get the framing right in the first place? • Is the female leader coming to a first departmental or board meeting that you will be attending? How can you help them be prepared? It's documented that a large percentage of non-white young women have never had any engagement with the most senior leaders of organisations – is this the case in your company, and can you think about what you could do to prepare the leader for the meeting, including introducing them to the meeting chair in advance? • Could you be a good sounding board to assist the leader in making decisions? Could you help them in navigating the guidance in this book about whether a decision is more important for decision quality or for acceptance?

3. Dealing with some of the early leadership challenges	• How are you valuing and rewarding your female leaders? Do you have a performance management system that is skewed towards rewarding male attributes? • Have you ever underestimated a female leader? If you have had a chance to consider the relevant section of this book, how do you think this would make them feel? What can you do to praise and demonstrate appropriate respect to your staff? • Do you recognise and talk about imposter syndrome where it happens in the organisation? Is it acknowledged that this is something that's felt widely by both men and women? What infrastructure do you have in place to build confidence among female leaders? • Be alert to any potentially innocent but inappropriate or overly personal questions that might be experienced by your female leaders. Be sure to role model the right behaviours with colleagues and address any issues that you're aware of.
4. Leadership tactics	• Have you had to tackle confrontation with a female leader in your organisation? Have you considered applying the framework in this book to ensure that you aim for the best possible outcome? • Are you a good network builder? Could you share your tips and experience with female leaders to make them more comfortable with this important aspect of the role? • What could you share with female colleagues about how you handle dissenters and disruptors? • Do you have effective methods you could share for prioritisation and delegation?
5. Managing others	• Managing staff is one of the most time-consuming and potentially challenging elements of a leadership role. What have you learnt that you might be able to share? • Are there any important meetings that your newly promoted female leader is chairing that you might be able to support with or observe to give some coaching on any areas for improvement?

6. Essential leadership skills	• What is your approach to negotiation? What are the most effective methods that you have applied and can you share examples? • What is the organisation's approach towards creativity and innovation? Are there appropriate tools in place for leaders to be effective in this area? • What mechanisms do you have to manage employee wellbeing? Have you looked at any underlying issues of sickness related to organisational stress? Does your organisation have an employee assistance programme?
7. Your role in the context of organ- isational leadership	• Where appropriate, do you share with other leaders the perspective that you have overall in terms of the organisational analysis that you conduct and how it might have a bearing on the team? Are you sharing learning and insight that would situate the work female leaders are doing within the wider organisa- tional context? • Do your organisational values feel inclusive for the whole workforce? Have you tested how they are received by female leaders and colleagues?

There are many other considerations that you might want to explore, but I hope these questions and reflections help both male and female senior leaders to test whether they are suitably supporting female leaders and setting the right conditions for their success.

I wanted to share two different perspectives from male leaders I greatly admire who are both highly considerate of their workforce and their impact as leaders, and who I am certain nurture talent in their organisations:

It feels like the worst thing I could do would be to offer advice on leadership. Not only would that take me straight into mansplaining territory, I think leadership is really personal so, instead, I will focus on what I've learnt, as I feel I still have to learn about leadership, rather than attempt to offer advice to you. To be honest, I feel as if I know less and less about leadership each week. I think that's partly because I'm very actively trying to unlearn a lot of what I saw leaders do in the late 1990s and early 2000s, almost all of whom were straight white cis non-disabled men. It's also because I feel less confident in what I used to be certain of and hopefully, therefore, am much more open to listening and learning. I'm trying to actively believe that everyone is doing their best – when I succeed in doing this, I find it really shifts my perspective. I think I need to get out of the way more by saying less, deploying others into visible or traditional leadership opportunities to speak or represent the organisation. My ambition is to do less as a leader and to learn more.
James Watson-O'Neil, CEO, Sign Health

Nurturing talent and leading an organisation is undeniably a multifaceted and dynamic process, demanding a harmonious blend of personal development, strategic thinking, effective communication and emotional intelligence. As a CEO (or a senior leader), your role transcends the conventional boundaries of management, venturing into the realms of inspiration, guidance and mentorship. Your role as the CEO, or a senior leader, is to create a nurturing environment where talent can develop and thrive. This involves being more than just a manager; it is about being a visionary, a communicator, a strategist, and, most importantly, an empathetic leader. By blending these skills, you create a culture where innovation flourishes, teams are motivated and the organisation thrives.

Rob May, author and leader at the forefront of the technology industry for the past 35 years

Final reflections

I hope you have enjoyed reading this book as much as I have enjoyed writing it. Once I started, I couldn't stop. It flowed easily because I had wanted to write this for so long. I hope it has given you some new ideas and insights about how you might handle your leadership journey or it might have just confirmed some of what you already knew, which has given you greater confidence that you are on the right path.

Whatever the circumstances, my desire for you is that you're able to go out and be the best leader you can be. If you have enjoyed this book and found it useful, spread the word – our biggest issues as female leaders are both our lack of belief in our ability to lead and the generally held view that still recognises men as the more effective leaders. We need more women to get the message that they can be fantastic leaders and feel part of a *lead with confidence* movement. Together, we can make a difference.

Enjoy your leadership journey.

A few words on female leadership challenges

At the outset I asserted my view that there is incorrectly not enough belief (including from women) that females can be great leaders. To explain why this might be the case, I wanted to include some further detail on what I see as being the key challenges women can face.

There aren't enough role models. Female leadership in business is relatively new (when you look back at the history of enterprise). There is less known about female leadership and fewer case studies and insights. In my career to date, there have been so few female role models that, if you're unlucky like me, you won't have had much opportunity to learn directly from those who went before. Fortunately, that is rapidly changing, but still, according to Statista, as of 2022, only 9 of the FTSE 100 and 21 of the FTSE 250 company CEOs were women.

Research suggests male traits are associated with more effective leadership capabilities. According to Tom Jacobs in *Pacific Standard* magazine, drawing on research by Andrea C Vial and Jaime L Napier, 'When defining an effective leader, traditionally, feminine characteristics are considered secondary to attributes like assertiveness.' Since many still associate 'effective leadership' with masculine traits, there is work to do to demonstrate how female leaders help a company be highly effective and successful. What is frustrating is that there is a growing evidence base that supports the argument that women are phenomenally successful leaders. As reported by John Henley in the *Guardian* in late 2020, based on analysis of 194 countries published by the Centre for Economic Policy Research and the World Economic Forum: 'Countries led by women had "systematically and significantly better" Covid-19 outcomes... locking down earlier and suffering half as many deaths on average as those led by men.'

The male–female power imbalance and long-held

prejudices have left women feeling vulnerable. Many female leaders have experienced prejudice or inappropriate behaviour in the workplace. In my early career, I was explicitly told, *'You're only here to take the minutes'* when I came up with a useful thought in what I had believed was an environment where contributions were welcome. A few months later, that same leader stopped me from contributing by putting his hand over my mouth when I was speaking. I reported him, of course, but it's a shame that it even happened. Alongside gender-based harassment and undermining, there's also an element of vulnerability for women in some work environments linked to power imbalances in both seniority and physicality, which can cause worry.

Women aren't seen as leaders in certain industries. It might be that some people just don't see women as leaders in some contexts, and it may be that this is because those industries are yet to see the change that other sectors have experienced with women rising through the ranks. When I attended a black-tie event as a senior manager working in a male-dominated industry, I would have made a small fortune if I'd received a payment every time one of the male senior leaders walked up to my male partner at the time, shook his hand and asked which division he worked in. This included leaders who really should have recognised me! Quite simply, due to the imbalance between male and female leaders, being an employee who was sufficiently senior enough to be invited and female put me in the minority.

To get ahead, some women have acted a part in order to succeed. Over the years, I have seen some high-achieving women operating in more male-dominated sectors displaying masculine traits and being 'one of the boys', and then in social purpose, charitable and public organisations, I've seen female leaders drawing strongly on their femininity to succeed. Again, as workplace enlightenment continues, this is thankfully becoming less of an issue. It is particularly important to role model authenticity, to open a door for others to feel they have no need to 'act a part'.

Framing how women behave is still a challenge. I'm aware that there is a positioning difference between a woman being labelled as ambitious – and the potential negative connotations of that association – and men being applauded for the same quality.

Assumptions about women's personal lives. Clearly, the lack of female leaders in CEO positions is partly a reflection of the career breaks that women take if they want to start a family. But you're not just penalised if you have children; assumptions can be made that *all women* might want to have a family at some point. This was demonstrated by a director who asked me years ago, '*Are you planning on having children?*' I said, '*I don't know, but certainly not at the moment*', and when I queried his question, he replied, '*We've been thinking about promoting you, but we wanted to make sure that you would be available and focused on the work.*' My perception is that you're not judged on your ability to be successful at work linked to your personal life in the same way if you are male.

I'm sure many minority leaders could share experiences and insights specifically on the issues of prejudice or inappropriate behaviour, and a great book which picks up on this and has a wealth of research on inequalities being experienced in the workplace is *Mind the Inclusion Gap* by Suzy Levy (2023), which I highly recommend.

Whatever your path to this point, you may have experienced one or more of these challenges and could continue to as we go through the rebalancing of gender roles in the workplace.

Despite these issues and some of the negative framing of these experiences, I want to strongly emphasise that leading a business or an organisation is a privilege and a hugely enjoyable endeavour, and I hope this book has helped you in thinking about and preparing for being a successful leader, with all the rewards it will bring.

References

Introduction
Brown, B (2018) *Dare to Lead*. Vermilion.
Ginger Leadership Communications. URL: uk.gingerleadershipcomms.com
The Gordon Cook Conversations. URL: gordoncookconversations.com
Society of Leadership Fellows. URL: stgeorgeshouse.org/society-leadership-fellows

1: Establishing yourself as a leader
Bartlett, S. *Diary of a CEO* podcast. URL: stevenbartlett.com/doac
Becker, B (2023) 'Leadership styles: the 11 most common and how to find your style [quiz]'. HubSpot.com 14 September. URL: blog.hubspot.com/marketing/leadership-styles
Bono, J E, Braddy, P W et al (2017) 'Dropped on the way to the top: gender and managerial detrailment'. *Personnel Psychology* 70.
Goleman, D (2000) 'Leadership that gets results'. *Harvard Business Review* March-April, pp 82–83.
Harvard Medical School (2012) 'The real-world benefits of strengthening your core'. *Harvard Health Publishing* 24 August. URL: health.harvard.edu/healthbeat/the-real-world-benefits-of-strengthening-your-core

International Coaching Federation (2024) 'Find a coach / mentor / supervisor'. URL: coachingfederation.org.uk/find-coach

Indeed Editorial Team (2023) 'Eight common leadership styles (plus how to find your own)'. *Indeed* 16 March. URL: indeed.com/career-advice/career-development/10-common-leadership-styles

Kay, K & Shipman, C (2014) *The Confidence Code: The science and art of self-assurance – what women should know.* HarperCollins.

Mayo Clinic Staff (2022) 'Core exercises: why you should strengthen your core muscles'. *Mayo Clinic* 22 September. URL: mayoclinic.org/healthy-lifestyle/fitness/in-depth/core-exercises/art-20044751

Sinek, S (2011) *Start with Why: How great leaders inspire everyone to take action.* Penguin.

2: Leadership in practice

Bailey, S & West, M (2022) 'What is compassionate leadership?'. *The King's Fund* 15 February. URL: kingsfund.org.uk/insight-and-analysis/long-reads/what-is-compassionate-leadership

'The nine Belbin team roles'. URL: belbin.com/about/belbin-team-roles

De Bono, Edward (1985) *Six Thinking Hats.* Little, Brown.

Meredith, J & Mantel, S (2006) *Project Management: A managerial approach.* John Wiley & Sons.

Myers–Briggs Company (2024) 'Myers–Briggs Type Indicator'. URL: themyersbriggs.com/en-US/Products-and-Services/Myers-Briggs

PRINCE2 certification: prince2.com

Robbins, S P (2002) *The Truth About Managing People.* Prentice Hall.

Toastmasters International. URL: toastmasters.org

Vroom, V H & Jago, A G (2007) 'The role of the

situation in leadership'. *American Psychologist* 62(1), pp 17–24. URL: web.mit.edu/curhan/www/docs/Articles/15341_Readings/Leadership/Vroom_Jago_2007_The_role_of_the_situtation_in_leadership.pdf

3: Dealing with some of the early leadership challenges

Chartered Institute of Personnel and Development. URL: cipd.org/uk

Tallon, M S (2016) *Leading Gracefully: A woman's guide to confident, authentic and effective leadership*. Highest Path Publishing.

Walters, T (2024) 'New research finds humility trumps arrogance in leadership success'. *University of Sussex* 20 March. URL: sussex.ac.uk/news/article/63987-new-research-finds-humility-trumps-arrogance-in-leadership-success

4: Leadership tactics

Bartlett, S (2023) *The Diary of a CEO: The 33 laws of business and life*. Ebury Edge.

Collins, B (2018) 'How to use the 4 Ds of effective time management'. *Forbes* 14 June. URL: forbes.com/sites/bryancollinseurope/2018/06/14/effective-time-management

Covey, S (1989) *The 7 Habits of Highly Effective People*. Free Press.

Matthew Hussey, 320 Media. URL: matthewhussey.com

5: Management of others

Scott, K (2017) *Radical Candor: Be a kick-ass boss without losing your humanity*. St Martin's Press.

Wajcman, J (2013) *Managing Like a Man: Women and men in corporate management*. John Wiley & Sons.

6: Essential leadership skills

Badaracco, J L (2002) *Leading Quietly: An unorthodox guide to doing the right thing.* Harvard Business Review Press.

Dannals, J E, Zlatev, J J et al (2021) 'The dynamics of gender and alternatives in negotiation'. *Journal of Applied Psychology* 106, pp 1655–72. URL: doi.org/10.1037/apl0000867

Elsesser, K (2021) 'Why women fall short in negotiations (it's not lack of skill)'. *Forbes* 21 January. URL: forbes.com/sites/kimelsesser/2021/01/21/why-women-fall-short-in-negotiations-its-not-lack-of-skill/?sh=42e255045d02

Kotter, J & Rathgeber, H (2005) *Our Iceberg Is Melting: Changing and succeeding under any conditions.* St Martin's Press.

Pearson, J (2024) *The Intuition Toolkit.* Simon & Shuster.

The Real Deal, PEAK Learning. URL: peaklearning.com/the-real-deal

7: Your role in the context of organisational leadership

Best Companies. URL: b.co.uk

Foster, R N (1986) *Innovation: The attacker's advantage.* Summit Books.

Kondratiev, N (1979 [1925]) 'The Major Economic Cycles'. *Review* 11(4), pp 579–62.

A few words on female leadership challenges

Clark, D (2024) 'Number of female CEOs at FTSE companies in the UK from 2016 to 2022' *Statista* 20 March. URL: www.statista.com/statistics/685208/number-of-female-ceo-positions-in-ftse-companies-uk

Garikipati, S & Kambhampati, U (2020) 'Leading the fight against the pandemic: Does gender "really" matter?'

SSRN 3 June. URL: papers.ssrn.com/sol3/papers.cfm?abstract_id=3617953

Henley, J (2020) 'Female-led countries handled coronavirus better, study suggests'. *The Guardian* 18 August. URL: theguardian.com/world/2020/aug/18/female-led-countries-handled-coronavirus-better-study-jacinda-ardern-angela-merkel

Levy, S (2023) *Mind the Inclusion Gap: How allies can bridge the divide between talking diversity and taking action*. Unbound.

Vial, A C & Napier, J L (2018) 'Unnecessary frills: Communality as a nice (but expendable) trait in leaders'. *Frontiers in Psychology* 15 October. URL: frontiersin.org/journals/psychology/articles/10.3389/fpsyg.2018.01866/full